Extraordinary Things
happen to
Ordinary People

Extraordinary Things happen to Ordinary People

THE AMAZING LIFE OF A PSYCHIC

CHRIS GUYON

Chris Guyon © 2013

ISBN 978-1-907203-64-0

Typesetting by Wordzworth Ltd
www.wordzworth.com

Cover design by Titanium Design Ltd
www.titaniumdesign.co.uk

Printed by Lightning Source UK
www.lightningsource.com

Cover image by Nigel Peace

LOCAL LEGEND

Published by Local Legend
www.local-legend.co.uk

To my daughters Rebecca and Cassandra,
two of the most beautiful souls I know.

Acknowledgements

I thank my parents Eileen and Bruce Allan for their loving encouragement throughout my life, and my 'soul sisters' Maggie Stanley and Pat Veck, always there for me through thick and thin.

My deepest thanks are for my soul mate and husband Tony, who recognised something special in me at the tender age of fifteen. He may not have always understood or agreed with what I did, but his love and support gave me the courage to explore the unknown.

I am grateful to my angels and guides who nudged me into writing down my experiences, and to my publisher Nigel Peace at Local Legend for all his help in making the book what it is today.

Previous Publications

Little Less Dragon, Little More Angel
(with Maggie Stanley)

AuthorHouse (2009) : ISBN 978-1-438994-95-6

Chris Guyon's website is *www.lovinggoodbyes.co.uk*

About this Book

Sometimes we all feel that we are just faces in a crowd.
Ordinary people. Nothing special.
We'll never be celebrities or prodigies, nor rich and famous.
But Chris Guyon teaches us that everyone is special,
for we are spiritual beings with wonderful minds
that can reach out for and touch the truly extraordinary.
By paying attention to the inner voice and opening our hearts
to the spirit world, we invite memories of past lives,
the development of psychic and healing gifts,
and the protection of angels.
This is the inspiring story of Chris Guyon's amazing life.

Contents

Introduction

One night I had a strange dream – well, I was taken out of it by an angel, who showed me to a room. The angel stood at the back to my right. In the middle of this small room was an oblong table with a chair facing it and sitting on the other side of the table were three beings in long white robes. They nodded for me to sit in the chair facing them. I did so and the one in the middle leaned forward and said, "You have cancer."

My first response was, "Please don't let it be the pancreas" as I was aware that this was a very painful way to die. The being shook his head and said, "It is unusual and it is deep, but all will be well," really emphasising those last four words. At that point the angel came over to me and once again I was back in my dream. I woke up the following morning wondering what on Earth that had been all about. I told my colleagues what had happened and they were horrified! They couldn't understand why I would have such a dream.

Four months later, I went to my doctor because I had developed a worrying condition on my foot which was causing me so much pain I was finding it difficult to walk. He referred me to the physiotherapy department at the hospital so that I could be shown certain exercises to relieve the pain. On my first visit, the very nice physiotherapist asked me to remove my shoes and socks so that she could see my feet. I noticed her frowning at a mark on my inner ankle. It looked just like a blood blister and I had wondered if I'd knocked my ankle with a shopping trolley. It didn't hurt and it didn't itch so I wasn't that bothered about it. The physiotherapist asked me if I had shown it to my doctor. I said that I hadn't so she strongly advised me to see him. She then showed me the exercises to help with my painful foot.

It turned out that my 'blood blister' was in fact a malignant melanoma (a dangerous form of skin cancer). I was warned that it was quite aggressive and that it was not of the normal type.

Everyone was shocked at my diagnosis but I remained calm. If the first part of the warning had turned out to be true then so would the rest: "All will be well." And it was. Here I am four years later telling you about it! People kept telling me at the time how brave I was, but bravery had nothing to do with it. Faith in what I had been told, that all would be well, helped carry me through that very dark time.

I am not afraid to die. Death has held no fear for me after my first angel experience at sixteen years old. I feel that I will be going home to a very loving environment.

Extraordinary things happen to ordinary people, and by sharing my story I hope it will help you to see the extraordinary in your own lives.

CHAPTER ONE

Many Lives

I felt such a pressure in my chest and such extremes of sadness that the only way to release it all was by crying. "Ah, you're such a sensitive child," said my mum as she ruffled my hair. I was seven years old and watching the Titanic sink in the black and white film A Night to Remember with my parents and younger brothers. It was the Sunday afternoon film on the TV. I had watched the film with interest until it reached the scene where the ship's lights go out and it starts to sink at an angle. Looking back, I realise how close to the truth she was.

The film was shown many times over the years but it always had the same effect on me. No matter what age I was, at exactly the same point in the film I would feel that pressure in my chest. It became a bit of a family joke and boxes of tissues were passed to me without anyone having to look at me. Then, one day when I was in my thirties, I had a flashback to a previous life. I was looking through the eyes of someone walking down a corridor. There were doors on either side with numbers on them. I could see the arm of the person who was walking down this corridor. It had a white sleeve and a white glove on the hand, carrying a silver tray with a glass of Martini on it. I saw another person approaching – a man in the same uniform, but he had his tray tucked under his arm. We nodded at each other as we passed – and then the flashback was gone.

I had a sense, a 'knowing' that I had been part of the staff on the Titanic and that was why I was so affected by that old film. The pressure in my chest was a memory of drowning... Over the years, I had other past life memories flash into my mind and the majority of them involved drowning, which may account for my fear of the sea in this lifetime. To be taken on a cruise would feel like a punishment to me. On our first holiday together, my husband suggested a romantic moonlit walk along the beach. I couldn't stand it after only five minutes. I could hear the sea whispering to me and I begged to be able to walk on the promenade!

I was shown another life but it seemed as though I was looking down from a great height on the scene below me, where I saw the mast of an Elizabethan ship and a man on the deck. He had sandy coloured hair and beard and I 'knew' he was me. He wore a white, open fronted shirt with breeches cut off at the knees, and he was barefoot. The ship was in dock and there were crowds of people on the quayside, come to see it off before it set sail. Amongst those there I saw a young woman with her mother and knew that this girl was the love of the man's life. I watched him jump from the deck down to the quayside to kiss her goodbye. In this flashback I felt all the emotions of this man as he kissed the girl he loved, but also a great sadness as he knew he would not be coming back from this voyage (it felt like a premonition). Then the ship's sails unfurled and caught in the breeze and it was time to leave. The man climbed back up onto the deck and waved to the girl quickly before taking his post on the ship. This had been such a powerfully emotional flashback.

Many years later, during a meditation I saw caves high up on a cliff face. In the valley below a wide river flowed rapidly. I watched as a caveman came out of the entrance of a cave and walk along a narrow path that led to the entrance of another cave. As I watched, I saw him stumble and then fall off the path and straight down into the rapid river. He was sucked under the water before any of the other cave dwellers saw it. I began to understand even more my dislike of water.

A while later, I attended a talk given by a Dutch Catholic bishop. I went with a friend, and in the break I went to get us a cup of tea; when I returned I saw that she was talking to the bishop. When she joined me after her chat, she told me that she'd been telling him about all my 'past life drownings'. She had asked him if he could suggest anything to help me and his reply was, "Tell her to stay away from water!" My mum once told me that when I was three or four years old I fell into a neighbour's fish pond while playing in their garden. Luckily, one of their sons found me and pulled me out quickly. Maybe water is trying to take me in this life? I made sure both of our daughters could swim from an early age!

I'm fascinated that the majority (well, those I've been made aware of so far) of the past lives I've had have been as men, but on one occasion I volunteered to be regressed as a demonstration to the rest of the psychic development circle I belonged to at the time. This time I saw a room with a window and a table with a birthday cake on it that had some lit candles. There was a group of people – a man and a woman, an older woman, a young boy and a teenage-looking girl. I understood that they were a Jewish family and that it was the girl's sixteenth birthday. The grandmother told them to sing Happy Birthday very quietly so as not to draw attention to themselves, because German soldiers were outside in the street. I knew that I was the birthday girl, and the person regressing me asked me to walk over to the window and look outside. I did so and saw that we were in a tenement building about four floors up. It was night-time and there were German soldiers out on the street, stopping people and checking their papers. The building opposite looked like a factory with a lot of windows facing the street. I was then moved on in the regression and this time I saw myself as a machinist in the same factory. I had a friend who was also a machinist and her name was Dora. We made uniforms for the soldiers. I was then moved on again and this time I was in my mid-twenties and a hospital assistant. Wounded soldiers, both German and English, were brought in. I was standing next to the bed of an English soldier and I knew that we had fallen in love. It was then time to end the regression.

There was another regression in which I was a woman. My first scene was of a little hut in the forest where I lived. I was about fifteen years old with long black hair down to my waist and a long dress made of coarse material, tied at the waist with plaited wool. I was a herbalist and I made remedies from things in the forest. I remember seeing a deer by my side while gathering the natural ingredients needed for my potions. The townspeople would come and see me at night, so they wouldn't be seen by their neighbours! In the next scene I was married and working in the fields with my husband and three children. I was now living in the town with my family; but then my husband cut himself with a scythe and, no matter what potion or remedy I used, the cut became infected and he died. I was then taken to the time of my own death and found that I was back in my hut in the woods, surrounded by my three children and grandchildren. It was a peaceful death. This may explain my interest in natural cures and herbal remedies in this life. I am now feeling a pull towards learning to make my own.

All these visions have come to me quite naturally and unexpectedly. They are very real. If I have had many past lives, then so have you!

When I moved to Somerset, I rented a house that was about three hundred years old, and it was almost opposite the parish church which was over eight hundred years old. There were a few shops on that side of the road too, including a newsagent's and next door to it a little restaurant. About a year after I moved there I had a strange regression experience. I was a young girl, about sixteen, with blonde hair tied up on top of my head and wearing a long dress that looked pale yellow with little flowers on it. I was living in the same house that I was living in then although the rooms were set out differently and one had a big oak table with pewter dishes set out on it. I lived with my widowed mother who was a dressmaker and I had a strong feeling that she was connected to the Huguenots who came over from France. In the next scene, my mother had sent me over the road to the haberdashery shop to buy her some more lace that she needed for a dress she was making. I watched as I came out of the front door, crossed over the lane and went into the little shop.

The next scene I saw was my wedding day. I was in the same house as before with flowers in my hair, a small posy of flowers in my hands and with a cream muslin dress on. I walked over to the church on my own and waiting for me was a man who looked very much like my local butcher today! He had a ruddy complexion and big mutton sideburns. I was then moved on to my death bed scene. My children were there and so was the doctor, who had diagnosed I had smallpox. Then I was brought back from the regression.

When I told the group I was with what I had seen, they gasped and then told me that the little restaurant over the road had once been a haberdashery shop. This confirmed to me that I had lived in this town before.

Past life regressions can sometimes throw up some interesting things. My friend and I once went to observe a hypnotherapy training group and part of the training was past life regression. I just knew before we arrived that I would not be chosen as a subject and I was proved right. My friend, however, was chosen. It was a very weird experience watching her as she was trying to make sense of what was going on. Although she could talk to us, she wasn't able to answer any of the questions asked by the tutor. Then she started to try to rub her hands together but they were becoming claw-like and very painful. At this point the tutor brought her out of the regression. My friend explained that, although she could see her surroundings, she was a deaf mute and so was unable to answer the questions asked by the tutor because she had never heard her name or where she lived! She told us that she had been in a hot country and that she was hiding among bushes to avoid being seen by the people who passed by now and again. She was starving and about ten years old. Further on from where she was hiding she found a wood and in the middle of it was a leper colony. She was allowed to join them but had to earn her food and shelter, so she was almost like a slave. My friend saw herself changing filthy straw where the lepers slept, and cooking their food and doing all the hard chores. She also developed leprosy herself and it was eating away at her hands, hence the pain in the regression. She was aware that as a deaf mute she was an outcast even in the leper colony.

Of course, there is no way of knowing how true these lives were. All I can say is that they have felt absolutely real to me – I recognised myself!

CHAPTER TWO

Angels

When I was sixteen I had just started working as a dental assistant. My parents had decided to go on holiday, just taking my younger brothers, leaving me behind with my other brother who was fifteen and revising for his CSE exams. My parents felt we were old enough to look after ourselves for a week and they trusted us. We had a family dog, a Labrador cross called Sam, so Mum and Dad knew that Sam would protect us. This was in the days of no mobile 'phones or Internet to keep in touch!

Our house was semi-detached with a lane that ran down the side of the house leading to Dad's garage. My bedroom was the 'box room' and the window looked over the lane, while my brother shared the back bedroom whose window looked out on the garden. The first night my parents were away, the dog started to growl downstairs. My brother knocked on my door to ask if I knew why Sam was growling. I said it was probably a cat that had wandered down the lane and told him to go back to bed, but I spent the rest of the night listening to the creaks and little noises of the house. This continued for the next three nights and the lack of sleep was making me begin to feel ill. I kept nodding off during work which was annoying the dentist; it didn't help when I was woken by the shrieks of the patient in the chair - the sucker tip had slipped from the corner of her mouth into her ear! From then on the dentist kept spraying me with water from his drill to keep me awake.

On the fourth night I lay in bed, in the dark, with my eyes closed but wide awake. I was just so desperate to get some proper sleep and in my head I was saying, "Please, please, I need some proper sleep. I can't go on like this for another week." All I know is that it was heartfelt plea, but I didn't know to whom. Then suddenly my room began to glow with a golden light. It was so bright I could see it through my closed eyelids, and to this day I regret not opening my eyes to see what was causing it.

Then I heard a voice say, "Sleep little one, we are watching over you. Sleep, you are safe." The gold light filled every part of my mind and body. I felt as if I was being held safe and that every cell of my body was filled with unconditional love. I know we humans talk about loving unconditionally but we are such a long way from the real thing. It was just such an emotional experience and I felt truly blessed because I knew I had experienced an angel encounter. The gold light faded away but that wonderful feeling of being held and loved remained. I am not a religious person and hadn't attended a church in years, but at that moment I felt like leaping out of bed and running down to the nearest church to say 'thank you'. Then I realised it was gone midnight and that it wasn't such a good idea to be running around at night on my own!

I didn't tell a soul about my experience – it was just too personal and special. I felt that if I talked about it I would lose that feeling of unconditional love. So, years went by and it was my own special secret. When I had been married for about two years, I finally shared what happened that night with my husband. He actually seemed a bit envious. He was a lapsed Roman Catholic and said that if something like that had happened to him he might

10

get his faith back. A few months later I then shared the experience with my best friend and she also thought it was amazing. It took a while but then I realised that the angels actually *wanted* me to share this with others, to let people know that they do exist and communicate with us.

Eleven years after that event I had booked to go on a Colour and Psychic weekend workshop. Before I went, our fourteen year old daughter had to have blood tests to see if she had Lupus or leukaemia. The results were not due until the following week so it was a very anxious time for all the family. On the first day of the workshop, there were seven of us and the two tutors; one was a psychic and the other was training to be a doctor of herbal medicine. The psychic lady had laid out coloured silk squares on the floor and placed crystals around the centre with a candle burning right in the middle. She had also laid face down, in a circle on the outer edge of the silk squares, angel oracle cards. She then asked us to hold a question in our heads that needed an answer and then randomly to pick one of the cards and sit back down without looking at the card. Of course, my anxiety about our daughter was uppermost in my mind and so I asked in my head if she would she be all right. We were then told to look at our cards and as I turned mine over it made me gasp: it was the Angel of Children card and the word on it was 'Trust'. I knew in my heart then that our daughter would be fine. I felt such a sense of relief; thankfully a week later we were told that she had the all-clear on those tests and it turned out to be something less threatening.

I just knew I had to buy a set of these cards for my own use and so a few weeks later they arrived. They were a revelation to me. I never looked at the book that came with them, which gave the meaning of each card, as I intuitively knew what the cards meant for each person.

I started practising giving readings, using those beautiful cards and my own intuition. At that time I was working as a nursing assistant at a Minor Injury Unit. Sometimes I worked a twelve-hour shift and if it was quiet I would get out my angel cards and give readings to the nurses. One day a colleague asked me how much I charged for a reading. I said I didn't charge. She then asked how much I would charge to go to her house and give a reading for herself and her cousin. Charge? I didn't charge because the practice helped me tune into the angels more and helped my confidence grow. I said that I'd be happy to come to her house but it would be free; she responded that my time was as important as anyone else's and again asked how much I would charge. So I said £5 each to cover the cost of the petrol. She was happy with this and on the arranged day I was really nervous, but the cards didn't let me down and I had two very happy ladies.

After a few weeks went by I had a strong feeling that the angels actually wanted me to spread the word that they existed and I received the idea of giving Angel Card parties at people's homes. I wasn't too sure if this would work, but to my surprise it took off by word of mouth recommendations. I met some lovely people during this time and the angels never failed me with the information they gave me through the cards.

It was around this time that Robbie Williams had released his song Angels, which I thought was very appropriate! I would hear it on the radio in my car while driving to these angel parties and in my head I would be asking the angels to be with me at the readings and to give me a sign - then Angels would invariably come on the radio. I was a bit slow catching on that this *was* their sign! It would make me laugh to myself every time it happened.

Then, one day I was driving to a party and asking the angels for a sign that they were with me, but nothing happened. No Robbie on the radio. I was really surprised and a little concerned. Had they decided to leave me on my own tonight? I arrived at the hostess's house and found that her two friends had already arrived. We were all in the kitchen while she made a cup of tea and I was just listening to the two friends chat, still feeling concerned that there was no sign from the angels. Then my ears pricked up as one said to the other, "Did you see Robbie Williams at Knebworth?" Her friend replied, "No, we watched it on TV because we couldn't get tickets." The first woman said, "Oh, we were there but my boyfriend made us leave before the end to avoid all the traffic. Can you tell me, did he sing Angels?" and the other replied, "Yes, he did." Well, I nearly choked on my cup of tea - there was my sign from the angels that they were with me, but done in a playful way.

A few years later I was on my way to a client who lived on a new housing estate that was still being built. I had looked on the developer's map to give me some idea of where she was and then set off to find her. I had driven to the area but there was a confusing sign that showed two different names of roads but no arrow to indicate which was which. I sat at this junction and asked the angels which way should I turn, left or right? I felt a slight pull on the steering wheel to the right, so right I went. The car radio was on and as I drove slowly down the newly-built road I asked the angels for a sign that I was near to where my client lived. At that exact moment Robbie started to sing Angels on the radio and I pulled the car over, singing along at the top of my voice and laughing at the same time because this was my sign. When the song ended I got out of my car and walked up to a small block of private flats, pressed the intercom and my client answered! When I saw her she said that I was the first person to have found her without ringing for directions once I entered the estate.

After my experiences at that original workshop I became interested in other courses. I went to a conference for alternative therapies and attended an angel workshop. This was the first time I had realised that other people knew about them too. There were about a dozen of us that afternoon, men and women. The lady running the workshop was lovely. She asked how many of us had experienced angel energy and I put my hand up along with a few others. She then told us how she had got to know them. Then she asked how many people asked their Parking Angel for help... A few people put their hands up, laughing, but I was puzzled – Parking

Angels? She went on to explain that angels can be asked for help in any situation and if you really needed to park outside a doctor's or near a particular shop, for example, it was fine to ask your Parking Angel. To be honest I found this a bit weird but the people who'd put their hands up were laughing and saying it was true. They then gave some instances of when this had happened for them.

The lady taking the workshop said that those of us who hadn't asked their Parking Angel for help before should give it a try when we got home. But, she said, they can't interfere with our free will. She described a scene for us of a busy High Street bustling with people. Every person was thinking about a problem or a worry, for example the boss was coming for dinner and they were worrying over what to cook, or not knowing if they should apply for a new job, and so on. She then described the angels that walked behind every person on that High Street, how they were wringing their hands and saying, "Please, please ask me! I can open your cook book to the right dinner. I can help you choose your next job." But unless those people asked their angel for help they couldn't intervene. This produced such a powerful image to me, of all those poor angels frustratingly wringing their hands, wanting to help but unable to.

Once I was home again I mentioned what I had been told to my husband who was shocked that I should believe such nonsense! The following day I had to go into the small town nearby and wanted to park outside the library. This town had a one-way system and it was usually impossible to park where you wanted to because other people had parked there first. On this occasion though, as I was about to turn into the one-way system where the library was, I thought I would ask my Parking Angel for help. I visualised exactly where I wanted to park and asked for the space to be made. As I turned into the road I could see cars parked all along the side of the library, but just as I was coming up to it a car that was parked right outside pulled away and I slipped into the space. There must have been a few shoppers who thought I was crazy for sitting in my car and laughing my head off for no apparent reason.

Angels

It was confirmation of what I'd been told. That evening I told my husband what had happened and he said it was just a coincidence, but I knew otherwise.

Then one day, while on holiday with my husband and daughters, we went to a local seaside town at the height of the tourist season. Unfortunately the car parks were full and my husband was getting fed up trying to find a space and the girls were getting bored, so I asked my husband if he wanted me to ask my Parking Angel to help. The girls got excited at this and grudgingly he said "Ok". So I asked my Parking Angel to find us a space at the next car park (which we already knew was full after trying there earlier). As we approached it we could see that it was still full and my husband was about to drive past when I told him to stop as a space was coming up. As he did so, a man came out from nowhere and got into one of the cars. As he drove out, we drove into the space. I was so happy that the angels had shown my husband they were real.

The girls were also excited and kept saying, "Daddy, say thank you to the angel." My husband laughed as he got out of the car and at that exact moment a single white feather floated down out of the sky and slowly wafted through the air, finally landing on top of his shoe! We all looked stunned at the feather and then my husband quietly said, "Thank you."

CHAPTER THREE

The Healing Path

I have always been a tactile person and would pat friends on the arm or back occasionally while talking with them. After a while, this seemed to be having an effect on them. Friends would say, "Wow, what did you just do?" and I would look at them, puzzled, and say "Nothing!" They would look confused and say, "It's feeling better now." This happened on a regular basis and I had no idea what I was doing. Then it got to be that I would only have to think about someone who was unwell and my hands would heat up…

I truly believed I was at risk of spontaneous human combustion then, because it felt as if I would explode with all that energy. Sometimes I'd say to my husband, "Quick, I need to discharge." I'd place my hands on his back and he would jump and say, "Bloody hell, what was that?"

I'd say, "I don't know, but I feel better now!"

I then started to wonder if all this heat was the start of the menopause so I went to see my doctor, who almost laughed me out of the surgery. He told me I was too young and to come back in twenty years (but he did do blood tests and they all came back fine).

As the months went by I began to see several articles on something called Reiki but I didn't quite understand what it was and didn't pay much attention to it. Then one day a friend and I went to a Psychic Fair that was being held in our local pub. The aim of the Fair was to raise funds to send a local child to America for treatment. Neither of us had ever been to anything like this before and probably wouldn't have done so if it hadn't been for the sick child. We wandered around the stalls, not sure what we should be doing. But I felt drawn to a lady nicknamed Spider who read Tarot cards. I had never had a reading before and neither had my friend, so we decided to be brave and have one with her. I went first and she gave me a pack of cards to shuffle, asking me to choose seven cards and lay them face down. When I'd done this she turned them over and gasped, "You've picked the top cards of the pack - this is so unusual." She then gave me a different pack of Tarot cards and asked me to shuffle those and pick another seven cards, which I did. To her amazement, they were the same seven cards as in the previous pack!

She then started to tell me what these cards meant, and that she had "so much coming through" for me. What was it she could see in the cards, that I kept stepping to the brink of and then stepping back from? I said that I thought I might be a healer, and with that she gasped again and showed me that all the hairs on her arms had risen! She told me that I'd been a healer many times in past lives and it was calling me again in this life, so I should go to the local Spiritualist church and train as a healer with them.

Then it was time for my friend's reading so I went to sit on a row of chairs where the three next to me were empty. A few minutes later three women sat down there and from hearing them talk it turned out they were mediums at that very church. I was too shy to ask them any questions but I didn't think this was any coincidence...

So a few weeks later my friend arranged for us to go and observe a healing evening at the Spiritualist church. We sat right at the back so as not to intrude, and watched as people chose which team of healers to go to. The teams were placed around the church and consisted of a qualified healer and an apprentice. As we watched, I felt drawn to the team at the front - a man who looked like he was in his late sixties with a lovely white beard and very kind face, and a younger man in his forties with dark hair. I thought to myself that if I ever wanted healing I would go to them. My friend and I became so engrossed in what was going on that we didn't realise we were now the only two people in the room apart from the teams. The man with the white hair came up to me and asked if I would like some healing. I got a bit embarrassed and said I was only there to observe, as I'd been told I was a healer and I just wanted to see what happened. He laughed and said, "My dear, how can you possibly know what your client will feel if you don't have healing yourself?"

I couldn't argue with that so reluctantly I went with him to the chair where the younger man was waiting. To my astonishment, the older man was the probationary healer and the younger man was his mentor! I sat on the chair and they gave me healing. When they stopped I felt a little light-headed so I asked them a few questions about the training for healers at the Spiritualist church. I was told that it took three months and then I would go in front of a panel of healers to decide if I had passed the training. If I had, I would then be a probationer for three months before being allowed to work on my own. I came away feeling a bit queasy from the healing session and irritated with the system - I didn't need a panel telling me if I was a healer or not, as I was already doing it. I just wanted to know if what I was doing was safe.

A few months later the same friend, my husband and myself attended a local Psychic Fair held at the Civic Hall. Now, I've always had a 'thing' for young men with shoulder length hair, white cotton shirts and blue jeans (don't ask me why), and lo and behold there was a young man fitting that exact description on one of the stands. A sign on the wall next to him said 'Reiki'. It was that name popping up again and I was curious to find out about it, so much so that much to my husband's and friend's amusement I went over to talk to him. As I sat down he asked me if I would like some healing. I said I was fine, but I was interested in the word Reiki as it had popped up a few times in my life and I didn't know what it was. He looked at me and said, "But you're a healer."

I told him that other people had said that, but I didn't know what I was doing and I was concerned that I might do some harm. He looked me straight in the eyes and asked, "Do your hands get hot for no reason?" I agreed. Then he asked, "Do total strangers tell you their life stories and problems at the bus stop or in a shopping queue?" I replied, "All the time!" He said, "You're a Reiki healer. Reiki has found you, so now you need to find a teacher to show you how to use it. But don't worry, you won't do any harm."

Once I got home I looked up training courses on the Internet but many of them were held in the north and stretched over a long time. I didn't want to go so far away and for long periods of time while my daughters were still young. Ideally, I wanted to do both levels I and II in one weekend, near to where I lived. Then, one day, a magazine of complementary therapy courses was pushed through my letterbox - to this day I have no idea where it came from. As I leafed through it, a page fell open to the Reiki section. On this page was a photograph of a man's head and shoulders and I could just feel the love coming from his smile. As I read through the advertisement I saw that this man's first name was the same as my maiden name, and spelled exactly the same way. Another synchronicity! He was giving Reiki levels I and II courses in one weekend and in the next county to mine, so I just knew that this was my Reiki Master. I booked myself onto a course that was to be run in a few months' time.

When the date came I was so nervous because I wasn't sure what to expect or how many people would be there. I had booked into a local B & B and it turned out that I was the only guest that weekend, but the landlady was lovely and kept me company at breakfast. She offered me a brandy to calm my nerves before I left but I didn't think that would go down too well, turning up smelling of alcohol…

The training venue was on the eighth floor of a local block of flats and my heart was banging when I knocked on the door. A lady answered it and introduced herself as Maggie, another student. Then more people started to arrive and in total there were six of us, four women and two men. Finally the Reiki Master arrived and apologised for being late - he had been giving healing to a neighbour who'd had a fall. We settled down in the living room with our notebooks and pens at the ready and listened to him explain what Reiki was and the kinds of situations it could be used in. Maggie and I were sitting together and we just hit it off straight away. We kept finishing each other's sentences, had the same sense of humour and laughed a lot. At one point the Reiki Master jokingly threatened to split us up!

I was fascinated by what he was teaching us and when it came to our first attunement (this is when the Reiki Master connects you to the Reiki energy) I had a wonderful experience, hearing a voice say to me three times, "You will give service." When I mentioned this to the Reiki Master afterwards he looked surprised and asked me if I had read the history of Reiki (I hadn't) because this is what Mrs Takata[1] had heard as she lay on the operating table, before leaving to seek out Reiki herself. I was very surprised, to say the least.

Towards the end of the first day, the Reiki Master presented us with the three main symbols used in Reiki and their Japanese names. Learning them was to be our homework for the night and we would be tested in the morning. If we got any of the symbols or names wrong, we would not pass the second level. This came as a shock to me – I hadn't expected homework or to have a test, and I began to panic.

All six of us decided to go to a local restaurant for dinner and to talk about the day. I admitted that I was really worried about

---

[1]   Mrs Hawayo Takata was born in Hawaii of Japanese immigrants. On a visit to Japan she was admitted to hospital for surgery but, the story goes, heard a voice telling her that it was unnecessary. A sympathetic doctor suggested Reiki, which cured her. She was then only the second woman to be attuned to Reiki, returning home in 1936 to promote this form of healing in the USA.

making a mistake with the symbols, especially the most complicated one. One of the men tried to break it down for me, to make it less daunting, but it only seemed even more confusing. I went back to my room at the B & B that evening and sat down, trying to draw the symbols correctly and pronounce their Japanese names. Page after page got screwed up and thrown into the bin as I kept making mistakes. It was now 11 p.m. and I thought, "This is ridiculous. I need to sleep because tomorrow is going to be an important day." I closed my eyes and sent out a plea to my angels to help me draw the symbols correctly in the test.

At 3 a.m. I was awoken with a start. There, floating above me, was a disembodied hand holding a large quill. As I watched, the hand drew the first symbol in the air with the quill and did so by numbers. Then it lay the quill down (although still hovering in the air above me). Once it 'knew' I had followed what it was doing, it picked up the quill and did exactly the same for the second symbol, and then the third. When I had taken in what had been done, the hand disappeared. I thanked the angels and went back to sleep a lot calmer.

In the morning I was feeling a little nervous about the test but looking forward to meeting up with Maggie again. The Reiki Master tested us first thing and to everyone's amazement, including my own, I drew all three symbols perfectly. Luckily we all passed the test.

Soon it was time for the second attunement. As the Reiki Master gently tapped my third eye it felt as if something was burrowing into my brain, and when he tapped the palms of my hands it felt like something very ancient was slowly opening up. Afterwards, I opened my eyes but my vision seemed misty. Then I realised that it wasn't my eyes – there actually was a white mist in front of me. One by one we were asked what we had felt or seen during the attunement, and when it was my turn I explained about the white mist in front of me. At this the Reiki Master's jaw dropped in amazement and he told me that a white mist denotes the presence of God...

After we had all shared our experiences, we finished the afternoon by taking notes of the information we were being given. I noticed a little rainbow on my page and looked to see where it could be coming from - it was a cloudy day and there were no crystals on the window ledges that would refract the light. I thought this was strange so I quietly asked the lady next to me if she could see it too. She nodded, and then the Reiki Master asked me if I noticed the rainbow - he told me that he had watched it play across my face for a while before it went onto my page.

The day came to a close and we all had a hug with the Reiki Master; when it was my turn he whispered in my ear, "You have a very special light, Chris, now go and shine it on the world." Maggie and I swapped 'phone numbers and addresses so that we could keep in touch and then it was back out into the world and everyday life. When I got home, I was so excited with what I had been taught about how to channel the energy through me.

I rang my mum and dad to tell them that I had passed. But while I was talking to my mum I could hear another woman's voice in the background, as if we had a crossed line. This shouldn't have been possible because the 'phone lines were fibre optic, but every time I spoke I was hearing this woman's voice. I kept stopping to try and hear what she was saying but could only catch certain words. I asked my mum if she could hear what was being said, but she said she couldn't hear anyone except me, and I kept stopping for no reason... This was getting even stranger but I carried on talking as best I could while trying to listen to the other woman. Then I heard her say, "Thank you for being Maggie's friend. She's had a rough time lately with... [she repeated in detail what Maggie herself had told me over the weekend]." I was flabbergasted. Who was this woman and how did she know about Maggie?

As soon as I said goodbye to my mum I 'phoned Maggie and told her what had just happened. She replied, "Hmm, I'm sorry but that was MY mum. She has a habit of coming through to my friends!" Her mum had died a few years ago but still communicated with people close to her.

This was something I hadn't expected to discover when I took a Reiki course!

CHAPTER FOUR

Reiki

I was so keen to let people know that I could help them using Reiki, but I just kept getting blank looks and being told they had never heard of it. Luckily my family and friends let me practise on them and all had to admit that they felt the energy as I used the methods taught by my Reiki Master.

Now, although I trusted what had been shown me, I was still a bit sceptical about the information regarding Reiki and broken bones. Apparently, when a bone is broken and set in plaster, it heals but not exactly edge-to-edge. New bone is made and we have a working limb again, but it is not 'perfect'. However, Reiki works on balancing energy wherever it is, so it will vibrate to bring the two edges together perfectly. The Reiki Master did warn us that this could be uncomfortable, even painful, for a day or so until the edges were in alignment. At that time I was working in a Minor Injury Unit, and I knew that once bones were set that was it. Oh, ye of little faith...

One day at work, one of the Nurse Practitioners started to develop a migraine and said she knew that she was going to end up lying in a darkened room for three days. I told her that I had trained in Reiki and asked if she would like me to give it a try. She was a bit dubious until I told her that all she had to do was sit down and close her eyes. After about fifteen minutes of channelling the energy, she gasped and said that her migraine had gone. This was the first time ever that it hadn't developed into a full-blown attack, but then she said that her shoulder was really hurting now - what had I done to her? I admit to a moment of panic, but then I actually 'heard' my Reiki Master's voice in my head, telling me to ask her if she had any old bone injuries from childhood. She thought for a moment and then remembered breaking her collar bone in a skiing accident as a teenager. I tentatively explained what I had been taught about bone injuries and said she should take her normal pain relief and all should be well in a day or two. Yet I was confused as to what had happened because my logical mind kept telling me it was impossible for a set bone to move.

Then a few weeks later I went to visit a friend and found that she was suffering from a blocked sinus and in a lot of pain. I offered to try Reiki and she willingly agreed. Within minutes, fluid started flowing from her nose and we had to grab a box of tissues! I was astonished that it had worked so quickly. She was so relieved, but then complained of her wrist aching. This time I didn't worry so much and asked if she had any old bone injury there. She thought for a moment and then said she had broken her wrist falling off her bike when she was a child, so again I explained to her what I had been told and recommended normal pain relief, saying it would be fine in a day or two.

A few days after this another friend came to see me and was interested in what I had learned. Although she had no physical problems at that time, she was feeling stressed so I offered Reiki to see if it would help. After half an hour I felt the energy stop flowing through me and my friend was very relaxed and calm, but she started complaining about a pain in her leg! I thought, "Oh no, here we go again." Then in my head I heard a voice that said, "You will now believe what you have been taught. Do not doubt again." It was not my Reiki Master's voice, but it was one I was to hear many times in the following years. So once again I asked my friend if she had any old bone injuries in that leg and was not surprised when she told me that she had had an accident when she was a teenager and had broken that leg. How could I doubt my training any longer?

Reiki became a very big part of my life and I was so grateful for it. As time went on I had people come to me for healing who had been recommended by friends and family. Eventually I gave up working at the Minor Injury Unit and started my own Reiki practice, and the 'phone never stopped ringing.

One day I received a call from a pensioners' group, asking if I gave talks about what I did. I was booked to be a speaker at their next meeting. About thirty people turned up on the day, their ages ranging from the late sixties to eighties. I felt a bit concerned that they may think Reiki was too 'New Age' for them. When I was introduced, I explained what Reiki was and one of the ladies sitting in the front said, "You mean you hypnotise people?" I quickly said "No" but the lady next to her said, "But you can put thoughts into people's minds?" Again I hastily explained that I didn't do that and went on to say that Reiki was not associated with any religion, at which point a lady at the back shouted, "Well dear, I am a staunch Christian and, if you don't believe in God, who do you give thanks to at the end of the day for this gift?" I said that I thanked the Reiki, as it had found me. To my surprise, other people then called out to the woman to be quiet and let me speak.

I asked if anyone wanted to volunteer to have a ten-minute taste of what Reiki felt like. The man who had been taking the minutes volunteered; so as he sat in his chair facing everyone, I stood behind him, closed my eyes, held my hands a few inches above his head and connected to the energy. I sent up a silent prayer of "Please don't desert me now!" After about ten minutes I opened my eyes and felt all thirty pairs of eyes looking at me... I could tell that the man had 'gone off to somewhere nice' during the ten minutes, because when he opened his eyes he wasn't too sure of where he was. A lady in the front leaned forward and asked him what it had felt like. He responded that he had felt a lot of heat, which I said was normal - it was the high vibration of the Reiki energy coming into his slower vibrating energy, and the heat felt was the friction of the two energies. He said he felt very relaxed, which again I said was quite normal and it was the very least that Reiki would do. But then he stood up and said, "I have something else to say." I now had visions of being dragged out onto the green outside and burnt at the stake. "Two years ago," he said, "I was in an accident and shattered my ankle bone. I've been in constant pain since then but it has now gone." A big gasp went up from everyone and I thanked Reiki for helping this man.

Afterwards I was brought a cup of tea and chocolate biscuits and given tickets for the raffle! Some people come over to ask if Reiki could help them with their ailments and I was also asked if I did home visits, so I gained two new clients – the man I had demonstrated on and the wife of a man who had watched. She couldn't come to the talk as she had a leg ulcer and was house-bound. I felt so humbled when I came away from there. I had gone in thinking that their age group would not be interested in Reiki and had been made to see that they were exactly the right group because they would benefit from Reiki the most.

After attending a course, I had decided to join the local Small Business Club. I had been the first Reiki person to be on this course and there were a few interesting moments as my work was so unusual. I'd been asked who my competitors were and I said "None" - it wouldn't matter if another Reiki person set up a practice right next door to mine as we would each attract our own clients. Who was my 'target audience'? I laughed and said, "Every-one, man, woman, child, animal, plant!" One day the trainer said to me, "Chris, you scare me. You don't fit into any business model I know." I think it was a learning curve for both of us. When I had to give my presentation at the end of the course, I was in front of a panel consisting of a bank manager, a small business owner and the man who ran the course. After my presentation the bank manager said, "I'm not quite sure what Reiki is, but if I ever needed it I would come to you." At this the trainer said, "Book him before he leaves the room!" which made us laugh.

About six months later I was asked by him to be the guest speaker at the next meeting of the Small Business Club. I described my work and how it was a different kind of service that could be offered to the public. At the end of the meeting, as people filed out of the room, the trainer said that he was in need of my services. I asked, "What, now?" and he said "Yes." The last few people heard this and came back into the room to watch. I told him to sit on a chair and close his eyes, while I stood behind him facing the curious few. I connected to the Reiki energy and felt it flowing for about ten minutes before it slowed down and stopped. As he opened his eyes I recognised that faraway look and the relaxed features of his face. He said that he had felt as if he were floating out of the chair. In my head I heard the voice again, telling me to ask him if he had any old bone injuries. So I asked and he looked puzzled, but then he said, yes, a broken wrist a few years before. I told him that it might ache for a day or two but to take normal pain killers and the Reiki would make it a perfect edge-to-edge match.

The following month it was the annual Small Business Dinner. My husband came along as my guest and we were sitting at a table with some other members whom I had met on the course, when the trainer approached our table with the Mayor. He looked at me and said, "Here she is, our local witch." I asked him not to call me that but he continued talking to the Mayor: "I asked her to do some Reiki on me and she did, but afterwards she asked me if I had any old bone injuries. I told her I'd broken my wrist and she said it might be painful for a day or two. I thought she was mad. Bloody woman, two days later I was in agony!" The Mayor laughed and I asked the man if he wasn't glad that I warned him it might happen. They both laughed and walked away. But I'm still not sure I liked being introduced to the Mayor as a witch...

Through my Reiki practice I was privileged to meet many wonderful people, either as clients or fellow therapists. As my reputation grew, I became known as 'the Reiki lady' and I was asked to give demonstrations at local 'pamper evenings' which I thoroughly enjoyed. It was wonderful to have people who knew nothing about Reiki happy to sit on my chair and give it a go.

As I have mentioned the chair, I suppose I'd better explain why I use that rather than a couch. My Reiki Master taught us to "Be like the Martini girls – any time, any place, anywhere."[2] He told us that in an emergency it was quicker for someone to find a chair than a therapy table. I prefer to give Reiki with people sitting in a comfortable armchair as that lets them be totally in control. If at any time they feel uncomfortable they can just stand up and walk out – not so easy if you are lying on a therapy couch. Thankfully that has never happened in the fifteen years I've been practising.

One day I received a call from my local council. They were trying to reduce the number of sick days taken by staff and had come up with the idea of bringing in complementary therapists one day each month. The council staff could book twenty minute sessions with whomever they chose, and had permission to leave their desks for that. These sessions would be free to staff and the council would pay the therapists. I thought this was a brilliant idea and so became one of the therapy team along with a homeopath, a reflexologist, a masseur and an Indian head masseur. On the first day the Leader of the council came to see us before we started and said they would trial this for three months and then get feedback from the Occupational Health officers. We were booked solid all day. It was so busy but a wonderful atmosphere, with all five of us working in the same meeting room, spread out around the walls. The lady who had contacted me stayed in the room to make sure everything went smoothly, and I could feel her watching me throughout the day. When she came over to me later I asked her if

---

2   A reference to a television advertisement of several years ago.

she would like to book me for the last session of the day, because I could see she was getting quite stressed. She reluctantly agreed, so when the other therapists were packing away I sat this lady down on my chair, asked her to close her eyes and then channelled the Reiki energy to her for about fifteen minutes. The look of amazement on her face when she opened her eyes was a picture. She told me that she'd been watching me during the day and thinking that just placing my hands around someone wouldn't have any effect, but then she had seen staff 'floating' back to their desks afterwards. Now that she'd felt the energy herself she apologised for thinking nothing would happen. From that day on we got on really well and she always made sure that she booked in with me for the last appointment of the day.

This scheme worked so well that the staff asked if the therapy team could come in more than once a month, so this was arranged on a fifty-fifty basis: the staff paid us for half of the appointment and we invoiced the council for the other half. One day I opened up the local Gazette newspaper and there was a big headline: 'Council Wasting Tax Payers' Money on Therapies'. To my horror, Reiki was the only therapy mentioned in the article. Thankfully the Leader of the council had said that these therapy days were cost effective by cutting the amount of sick leave. At the following month's therapy day, the Leader came to talk to us all and when he was introduced to me he said, "Ah, you're our trouble-maker", but thankfully he laughed it off.

One lady who came to see me every month was later sadly diagnosed with terminal cancer. Her colleagues were upset and came to see me one day; the lady was now off work and having chemotherapy, and her friends knew how much she had enjoyed her Reiki sessions. So instead of having a collection for flowers to send her, they asked if I would go to her house and give her Reiki there, which they would pay for. I was touched and agreed, as long as I could donate two sessions each month. It was an honour to be able to go to this lovely lady's home and to lessen the symptoms of her cancer and chemotherapy. She was a very brave lady right to the end and I had the honour of talking to her briefly on the telephone the day before she died. It made me extremely aware of how Reiki had brought me into people's lives.

Among all the very special experiences I've had with Reiki, there is one that stands out. Because of the Community Committee that my husband and I belonged to, we had contact with our local MP. One day she invited us all to come to Parliament for a tour. A coach took us to London and when we arrived at Parliament we were taken up a stone staircase to a reception room where drinks and nibbles were being served. The MP was already there with her husband and once everyone was there and had a drink in their hand she welcomed us all – but her voice was very croaky and she kept losing it. At this point my hands started to heat up and tingle and I knew that Reiki was ready to flow through.

I noticed the MP then sit down in a corner of the room, in a quieter space, not surrounded by people. As it happened, one of my Reiki students was also on this tour and I asked her to join me as I approached the MP and asked her if she was well enough to take us on this tour. She croaked that she would have to be, although she kept coughing while she was talking. I asked if she would like me to channel some Reiki to her. She looked a bit surprised and asked me what she would have to do. I explained that all she had to do was sit there with her eyes closed while my student and I sent her Reiki, so she looked relieved and agreed. My student stood in front of her and I stood behind with my hands resting lightly on her shoulders, feeling the energy start to flow. She started to relax and I could see her face soften; after ten minutes I gently told her we were finished.

When her eyes opened I could see that she wasn't quite 'back' yet so we quietly chatted to her as people began to move towards the door, ready for the tour. I asked if she felt ready to guide us on this tour and she jumped up with a very enthusiastic "Yes!" So off we all went, with the MP in front calling out the history of each room as we were shown around. After about forty minutes we were on our way back up the stone staircase when she turned around and said to me, "This Reiki stuff is brilliant isn't it?" She hadn't coughed or lost her voice the whole time we were being shown around. As I look back to that time, I feel quite excited that my student and I had given Reiki to an MP in the Houses of Parliament.

CHAPTER FIVE

$$\mathcal{Spirit}$$

Although I am not a medium in the true sense of the word, I would sometimes have the spirit world coming through to me during a Reiki session. This is not a normal part of Reiki, I hasten to add, but I believe that they use the high vibration of the energy to come through.

One day I had a client whose husband had died suddenly in his late forties; she was grieving and in so much shock. We worked together on this issue for a month and although other health problems improved the shock was still the same. Around this time, I developed a slight limp in my left leg which made my hip and ankle hurt. I couldn't understand why as I had done nothing to have caused it. Then one evening, as I was watching TV with my husband, I developed a pain that started in my left arm and then into my chest; I continued watching the TV thinking I couldn't possibly be having a heart attack... We then went to bed but I just couldn't settle. If I lay on my back, the pain in my chest got worse, and if I lay on my right side then the pain was excruciating from my left side. I ended up propped up on my pillows, dozing.

In the morning my husband took one look at me and asked what was wrong. I hadn't told him about the pain as I hoped it would go away but now I said I wasn't sure if I should call the doctor or go to hospital. With that he rang a neighbour and asked them to keep an eye on the girls while he rushed me straight to hospital. I was taken into A&E and put on heart monitors because they were sure I was having a heart attack, but after half an hour they checked the monitor and it showed that my heart was fine. They couldn't understand what was going on so they asked me if I had fallen in the last few days or had a chest infection. I could answer "No" to all of it. They took my blood pressure and were concerned that it was high, insisted that I saw my GP the next day and then sent me home with pain killers.

Although I had been in a lot of pain, I had known it wasn't my heart. But then it suddenly occurred to me that my client's dead husband, who had died suddenly of a heart attack, had given me his symptoms so that I would know it was him. He wanted to be with me because he knew his wife came to me, and he wanted me to tell her that he was all right, and sorry that he had left her so suddenly.

I wasn't too keen on having his spirit attached to me but it just so happened that I was attending a Reiki training weekend with Maggie the following week. My Reiki Master would be there so I could ask him what I should do to 'move this spirit on'. I hadn't mentioned any of this to my husband or daughters as I didn't want to worry them.

Meanwhile, when I picked up my eldest daughter from a party one evening (she was seventeen) she said to me, "Mum, I think I'm going mad. I keep seeing a man looking at me in my room, but when I look straight at him he's gone. Now at college I keep hearing a man call my name, and it's happening at work too." I felt very guilty. Because I was blocking this man from my energy, he had latched onto my daughter whose energy centres were quite open. I told her not to worry, I knew who he was and that I would be doing something about him at the course the following week. She seemed very relieved to hear this, especially when I told her she had the power to send him away from her. A few days later I asked her if everything was ok. She laughed and said that he had come to her again the night before but she had told him, "Bugger off, you're nothing to do with me. Go and see Mum!" and he had vanished. I did tell her not to be so disrespectful in future when talking to spirits!

The following weekend, Maggie and I were in London for the course. Emotions were quite intense in the morning and at one point it was unbearable; in my head I said, "Please, angels, protect me as I don't think I can take any more." At that point I felt angel wings fold around me from behind and I felt loved and safe. After that session Maggie said she had felt an unusual draught go by her (she had been sitting next to me) and I told her about the angel wings. She was amazed that she had felt their movement.

During the lunch break I asked my Reiki Master if he could 'move on' a soul and he said he could, but not normally on a course like this. I told him about my client's husband and he was fascinated, so after lunch he asked the group if anyone was interested in 'soul retrieval'. Every hand went up and he laughed as he looked at me and said, "Now I know why you are on this course!"

He told the rest of the group to go right to the back of the room, to give me space. I then had to bring my chair into the middle while he wrote down some questions on a notepad - these were questions that I had to ask the spirit. He warned those in the group with psychic gifts not to focus on what was going to happen in case the spirit was drawn to their energy. Everyone went very quiet and waited for us to start.

My Reiki Master told me to ask the spirit the questions he had written down and then I was to tell him the replies. I could see these in my mind. The spirit did not want to leave because he was worried about his wife and that she wasn't coping. He knew that she came to see me and that the Reiki energy helped him to connect to me. I promised him that I was doing everything I could to help his wife and that I would be referring her on to another trustworthy therapist who could help her even more. He seemed happy with that so my Reiki Master told me to visualise the colours of the seven chakras (centres of energy on a human body) and tell him to go through one of them. I could see 'doorways' of colour swirling in front of me and I urged the spirit to go through one of the doors, where loved ones were waiting to meet him and help him. I saw him go towards the orange door, turn to wave goodbye to me, and then he was gone.

When I said that I had seen this, there was a big sigh from the rest of the group and some were quite tearful. They had felt this spirit's energy and sadness. A few had seen him too but had not focussed on him. Maggie was also feeling quite emotional. She had seen his footprints on the carpet as he walked up to stand right behind me. She said he had been really close to me and when I had told him to go towards the doors he had squeezed my shoulder before he went. I felt lighter in my own energy again, and my Reiki Master thanked me for being a willing guinea pig for the rest of the group.

Obviously I had not mentioned any of this to my client, the widow, but on our last session I felt it was the right time to tell her that her husband did not want her to be so sad. As we sat facing each other, I held her hands between mine and sent her love and Reiki while I explained that her husband had been so worried about her. He wanted to tell her that he loved her very much and always would. She pulled her hands away from mine and demanded to know how I knew it was her husband. I told her about my 'heart attack' but she shook her head and said it could have been anyone. Then, for some unknown reason, I told her about everything on my left side that had gone wrong after she started coming to see me. She looked at me intently and asked what I meant, so I told her that my left hip hurt and that I had developed a slight limp, and so on. At this her hand flew to her mouth and she looked at me and nodded. Apparently he used to wear an old pair of trainers that he absolutely loved; but because the soles were worn down in places it made his balance slightly off, which resulted in a painful limp. I knew then that my work was done with this lady and happily referred her to a colleague who would be able to help her in other ways.

I was asked to do a home visit for a gentleman who was having problems with an ankle. On my first visit his daughter was in the house – obviously to make sure I didn't run off with the family silver. She stayed in the kitchen while my client and I sat in the lounge, and I asked him questions about his medical history. While we were talking the 'phone in the hallway started to ring but he ignored it. His daughter came out of the kitchen and picked up the 'phone, and as she was walking back to the kitchen I could hear her saying "Hello? Hello?" My client told me that this 'phone was an extension, but when anyone answered it there was no-one there. He had had the lines checked by the telephone company but they couldn't find a fault anywhere. The strangest thing was that the extension rang without the call going through the main 'phone.

During our session he told me that he had lost his wife three years earlier and I could tell he was still very angry about the way she died. He felt that the doctors had let her down with their diagnosis and treatment. I noticed that there were no photos of her anywhere in the room, which I thought was strange. After taking all his details we then started the Reiki. We made arrangements for me to come back the following week and during our chat - about how he had been since my last visit - I asked him if the 'phone had rung again. He said that it had, three times, but nobody was there. Again, nothing was coming through the main 'phone, only the extension. It then occurred to me that maybe this man's wife was trying to get through to him.

I wasn't quite sure if this was something I should mention at this stage of his treatment, but as he was a retired engineer I talked to him about the high vibration of Reiki which was similar to electricity, which he understood. When I saw him the following week his ankle was feeling much better, to our delight. In passing, I asked about the 'phone again and he told me that it had rung every day but, again, no-one was there. This was interesting as these events were happening on a regular basis now and I laughed, saying that it had escalated since I had started visiting…

I stood behind him and linked to the Reiki energy. In my mind I see it as a column of bright white light that comes down over my head and flows through me. When I opened my eyes, to my great surprise there was a lady standing next to me. She had brown curly hair, glasses and was a few inches shorter than me, in her sixties. In my head I asked her if she had come for the gentleman and she nodded, so I asked her if she had a message for him. Again she nodded and said, "It's time to move on. It's time to have FUN!" As I looked in front of me, I could actually see the word in capital letters. I asked her name and she said "Milly"[3] - then she was gone. I was so surprised but now had a dilemma: I was there to channel Reiki, not give messages from dead loved ones. What should I do? I worried for a few seconds and then realised I couldn't deny a spirit their message to a loved one. It had taken a lot of energy for her to materialise in front of me, using the Reiki vibration to do so. I decided to tread carefully and after the session I sat and had a cup of tea with the gentleman. During the conversation I asked about his wife, where did she work and so on? He told me a bit about her and it turned out that through her job they knew my parents, so I then felt it was time to tell him what I had seen.

I described her height, her brown curly hair and her glasses. He looked at me for a long moment, then got up from the sofa to walk over to a dresser where he pulled open a drawer and took something out. It was a photograph of a lady looking just as I had described her. He asked how I could possibly have known what she looked like. Then I asked him her name and he told me 'Morag'. Blast, wrong name! So I felt I couldn't give him the message. But as I thought this he then told me that her real name was Morag but he had always called her Milly! That was the confirmation I needed to make sure I had the right spirit and message.

---

[3] The names here have been changed, for the sake of privacy.

Gently, I explained that spirit energy is also of a high vibration and that sometimes they used Reiki to come through. I told him that this was not a part of Reiki but it sometimes happened to me during a session. I then said that I thought the extension 'phone ringing on its own was his wife, manipulating electricity to try and get his attention. He asked me what the message was, and I told him that she didn't want him still to be angry after all this time. It was time for him to move on and have some fun. He laughed at this and said that only the night before he had agreed to go on holiday with one of his sons and his family, the first holiday since his wife had died.

As we sat there, I told him that the next time the 'phone rang he should answer it and let her know that he had got her message. The very second I said this, the 'phone started to ring!

We both jumped and looked at each other, then he stood up and went into the hallway to pick up the 'phone. Sitting in the lounge I could feel tears welling up as I heard him speak to his beloved wife and tell her how much he loved and missed her. I kept blinking them back as I thought it wouldn't look very professional if the therapist was crying. He put the 'phone down and walked slowly back into the room and sat down, looked at me and said, "You couldn't have got the timing spot on even if you'd planned it!" I laughed and admitted to being pretty spooked myself. When I visited him the following week for our last Reiki session (his ankle had healed and he wasn't in any pain now), I asked him if the 'phone had rung anymore. He looked at me for a few moments and then told me that it hadn't rung once since that day. As I was leaving, he called out that when he next saw my parents he would tell them that he had met me, and he thought I was 'a spooky woman but nice'.

When I moved to the south-west, I felt that I wanted to put something into my new community and it just so happened that the local women's refuge were looking for all types of volunteers. So I contacted them and went along for a group interview. I was the only therapist and we arranged for me to go to the refuge once a fortnight to offer de-stressing Reiki sessions for the women who were there. The first two sessions were a bit slow but after that I was fully booked.

During the year I was there I met some amazing women and quite often someone from the spirit world would come through to give a message. One lady was quite 'spooky' herself and when she came into the room she looked at me and asked, "Who is the lady with you?" I wasn't aware of anyone behind me but the woman told me that the lady was giving me lots of sunflowers. I immediately knew who it was - a close friend of mine had died six months before and her favourite flowers were sunflowers, in fact she had a vase of them on the windowsill in the room where she died. I found it a great comfort to know that she was around me.

I have had so many instances where Reiki has popped up in my life in the most unexpected places. I have a column in a Reiki newsletter, called The Everyday Life of a Reiki Practitioner, in which I write about my experiences.

Once I had visited my local council office to pay my Council Tax. I arrived at the office too early so I decided to wait outside until it opened, and while I was waiting a security van pulled up; the security man tried opening the office door but I explained it wasn't open yet. Ten minutes later we heard someone on the other side of the door slowly unbolting it. A lady opened the door and apologised for being so slow, but said she had just returned to work after having an operation on her shoulder and it was still painful to use her arm. She let us both in and went back to her position behind a glass screen while the security man brought in money bags and took them through to the back office. While I wrote out my cheque for the Council Tax, my hands got hotter and hotter as I felt the Reiki energy flow through me. As I handed the lady my cheque I told her that I was a Reiki practitioner and asked if she would like some Reiki, to see if it helped her shoulder. To my surprise she agreed and told me that she had received Reiki once before. She then let me into the secure part of the office, where the security man was bringing in the money bags!

That was very surreal. There I was, standing behind the lady in a secure section of the office, channelling Reiki through my hands to her shoulder surrounded by money bags. After ten minutes I felt the energy begin to slow down and knew that the condition had been improved. The lady was amazed that the pain had gone so quickly.

Another time I had to see a financial advisor at my local bank and during our conversation it came up that I was a Reiki practitioner. He asked me what that was and when I told him he nodded his head and then looked for something in his briefcase. He pulled out a photograph of himself, sitting in a wheelchair wearing a tee-shirt and shorts. He told me that a year before he had been in a coma for three weeks and had an infection in his legs, and when he had come out of the coma the doctors had told him he might never walk again. He told me that it had been the devotion of his wife, who was five months pregnant at the time, that had enabled him to walk again. She would wheel him down the hospital corridors and help him to hold onto the wheelchair and slowly shuffle back to the ward. He then asked me a lot of questions about Reiki and wondered if it would help his mother-in-law. I came out of that meeting feeling a bit confused. Who would have thought that a meeting about finances would include being shown a photo of your financial advisor in a wheelchair and a discussion about Reiki?

Another time when Reiki popped up in an unexpected place was when a friend and I decided to go on a trip to Sedona, Arizona. My friend was very busy so asked me to make all the arrangements. I had booked everything except the shuttle from Flagstaff to Sedona, so I looked online for a shuttle company and one name seemed to glow on the screen. I emailed them with the dates and a lovely lady replied, so with relief I was able to tell my friend that everything was sorted. On the morning of being collected, my friend and I were having breakfast. As we finished, this same lovely lady walked into the foyer and straight over to us, calling us by our names. We knew straight away that she was the shuttle driver but wondered how she knew us, as we'd never met before. She gave each of us a big hug and welcomed us to Arizona. It was on the drive to Sedona that she told us she was a Mormon but also a Reiki practitioner, which then explained the link we had felt. It was as if we'd known each other for years.

At a friend's barbeque one summer, all her family and friends were outside in the sunshine but I saw her father in the kitchen. I had known him since I'd been at school so went in to say hello. He wasn't a tall man but I was surprised that he continued to look down at the floor while talking to me. He realised this and apologised for appearing rude, but explained that he had spondylitis in his neck which meant he couldn't lift his head up. He felt so embarrassed and miserable about it. I could feel my hands begin to warm up and asked him if he would like me to help. He agreed but wasn't sure what he had to do, so I told him to go and sit outside in the sun with everyone else and I would just place my hands lightly on his shoulders. I assured him people wouldn't notice what we were doing. He went outside and sat in a deck-chair near his family while I stood behind him with my hands resting lightly on his shoulders. He carried on talking to people while I just nodded if people included me in their conversation. I could feel the energy flowing into him and after a few minutes I watched in amazement as he gradually lifted his head until he was able to look straight ahead again. Bless him, he was so grateful and I was happy that Reiki was able to help him.

One year, my husband and I attended a business dinner and were sitting at a table with four other couples. During the first course we chatted and found out what our respective businesses were. My husband was sitting next to a lady who told us that she was a tour guide who took people on coach holidays and the like. She admitted that she was not looking forward to the nine-hour journey she was to make the next day because she had severe back pain. At this, my husband looked at me as if to say, "You're off duty now. Enjoy the meal." But when the main course was served I started to feel tingling in my hands and I knew it wasn't the wine.

In the end I had to ask this lady if she would like me to see if Reiki could help. She wasn't sure because she had never heard of Reiki and we were in the middle of eating a meal. I told her it could be done discreetly and would be easier if she swapped places with my husband, who raised his eyes to Heaven but got up and swapped with her. Sitting at a round table made things easier as I was able discreetly to put my hand on her lower back while she continued to eat her dessert. After fifteen minutes she was amazed that her back pain had gone, but that there was still a lot of heat there. Her husband gave me his after-dinner chocolate as a thank you!

Because my younger daughter felt strongly about certain things and was happy to be an active member in her community, she caught the attention of our local Labour councillor. He liked her drive for someone so young, and invited her to afternoon tea at his home to meet other members of the Labour Party. She was about fourteen at the time and happy to go as long as I could go with her. When we arrived at the councillor's home we were welcomed by his wife, who ushered us into the back sitting room. To our surprise, not only was the councillor there with some other people whom we didn't know, but also our local MP and her husband. Everyone made us feel at ease but as the discussion started I was aware of a lady sitting opposite me. Every time I looked up she was looking at me. I kept out of the discussion as I was just there as a chaperone for my daughter, but the MP was very impressed with what my daughter had to say (and from that day our whole family became friends with her and her husband).

When the meeting was over, several people left and there were just my daughter, myself and the lady who had been looking at me. She asked me what work I did and I answered that I was a Reiki practitioner. She then gave a big smile and said, "I knew there was something different about you. The energy in here completely changed when you walked into the room." From that afternoon we became friends and later she decided to take her Reiki level I course with me. I am happy to say that she went through all the levels to Master with me over the years and we still keep in touch.

CHAPTER SIX

Guides

As I continued on my spiritual path I became aware that not only did we have angels with us but also guides to help us. Because of all the experiences I was having of spirits coming through, I had wondered whether I should look for a psychic development circle to help me explore what was happening. I found out then that the universe works in wonderful ways...

When I decided to start up my Reiki practice I had attended a one day business workshop. This was all new to me, as I sat around a U-shaped table with other complete strangers of all ages, men and women. We did a breaking-the-ice exercise where we had to interview the person sitting next to us, and write six things about ourselves on a sheet of paper. I was in awe of the lady next to me for all the things she'd done, but as she started to interview me she kept writing everything down and saying, "Wow! That's amazing." After the interviews we then had to take it in turns to stand and tell the rest of the group about the person we had interviewed and stick up on the wall behind us what we had written.

I had noticed a man sitting diagonally across from me - a big chap with crew-cut hair and quite scary looking. He was setting up a business in training people to ride motorbikes and had recently qualified as an instructor. You can imagine how apprehensive I was when he approached me during the coffee break. He told me that he'd been interested to hear that I was a Reiki practitioner. His wife ran a psychic development circle and was waiting for one last person to join; he thought that person was me.

I was stunned. The universe had obviously heard my thoughts and had gone into action. Who would have thought that attending a business workshop would have connected me to a psychic development circle? Two weeks later I was on my way to this couple's house. I was a bit apprehensive because I didn't know what to expect, but there was also a spark of excitement. The circle consisted of the medium who ran it and five other women of varying ages. I was introduced to everyone and they all made me feel so welcome that I felt I belonged.

We went to sit around a table in the dining room and the medium led us in a meditation to meet our guides. In this we were to go into a garden and sit on a bench there, behind which was a gravel path leading up to a gate in the garden wall. We were to sit with our eyes closed and wait for our guide to join us. I dutifully sat on the bench in a very nice garden with my eyes closed, and I could hear the gravel start crunching as someone walked up the path towards me. In my mind I caught sight of the hem of a robe made of rough cloth, and glimpsed a pair of leather sandals. I immediately thought, "Oh great, a monk, how original," for which I am ashamed to this very day.

The medium told us to open our eyes - in the meditation - and see who was with us. I opened my eyes expecting to see a monk but instead I was looking straight into the eyes of Jesus. I was stunned as he sat down beside me on the bench in silence. I was racking my brains for something to say to him and all I could think of was, "Are you truly the son of God, or were you just a very good healer caught up in the politics of the time?" He smiled enigmatically at me but never uttered a word. Then I heard the medium asking us to thank our guides, because it was time to come back. Jesus stood up, smiled down at me and went back down the path.

I slowly opened my eyes, feeling slightly shocked by what I'd seen. Once we were all back from the meditation the medium asked each of us in turn to share what we had seen. I started to panic. I was the third person she was going to ask. The other two ladies before me had seen more 'familiar' guides. I started to go clammy at the thought of the new girl on the block telling them that she had seen Jesus!

The medium smiled at me and asked whom I had seen. I answered that I would rather not say, but she insisted that everyone shared what they saw in meditations. So I took a deep breath and said, "Well, I saw Jesus." This caused a slight gasp from the others, so I hastily added, "Well, it couldn't have been him because I'm not religious and don't go to church. And it even more couldn't have been him because he looked like the westernised version of him rather than the colour he would have been, dark skinned and with brown eyes." At this the medium laughed kindly and asked, had he come to me looking like Bruce Forsyth, would I have recognised him? I said of course I wouldn't, and she laughed again before saying that it was indeed Jesus and that he had come to me in a way that I would recognise. She then added that she had come into my meditation and seen him too. I was amazed, not only that I had seen Jesus but also that the medium could go into our meditations. This she proved by talking to the other ladies after me and telling them what she had seen in theirs, which they confirmed. I came home that night so full of energy after being with like-minded people. From then on I attended circle every week, right up until I moved to the south-west.

I have seen Jesus twice more during meditations over the years. The second time was when we were 'sent' to a tropical island where we would meet our guides. As I visualised this place, I saw him sitting on the sand with his back up against a palm tree, in the shade. I walked towards him and he smiled, then pointed out to the beach and water. I was puzzled, so I looked back at him and he pointed again and nodded at me to go out to the beach. I did so and as I got to the water's edge a beautiful dolphin swam towards me. I looked back at Jesus leaning against the palm tree and he smiled and nodded his head – yes, he wanted me to go with the dolphin.

Now remember, I have a fear of drowning and he laughed at the sight of my panic stricken face but still pointed to the dolphin. So I waded out into the water and climbed onto the dolphin's back and held on for dear life. The dolphin took off back out to sea with me clinging on, as the island got smaller and smaller, then suddenly dived down and down, taking me with it. I started to panic as I thought I was about to drown but when I couldn't hold my breath any longer I realised that I could breathe after all. I calmed down and started to enjoy the ride. The dolphin kept going deeper and deeper until I saw a faint glow coming from the bottom of the sea bed. As we got closer I saw that it was a ruin but it had clear walls made of crystal. Inside some of the buildings were men in white robes who looked like they were doing experiments. I then knew that this was Atlantis and that it still survived with its technology. It was fascinating looking at all that was going on as the dolphin weaved in and out of the ruins.

After a while the dolphin decided to take me back up to the surface. As we surfaced close to the tropical island, I saw Jesus laughing as I coughed and spluttered. I thanked the dolphin and then went up the beach to ask him why he'd done that. The reason, he told me, was to prove to me that I was not to live in fear. What appears to be scary isn't necessarily so. That's a philosophy I have adopted in my everyday life.

The last time I saw him was in a meditation where we were both sitting on a high cliff, our feet dangling over the edge, and watching the sun set over the sea. It was very peaceful and such a beautiful sight.

I have often wondered if there is any significance in my being named Christine! With my 'soul sister' Pat on our drive down to Somerset for a healing festival one year, we discussed the belief that Jesus didn't die on the cross but was given a drug that made him appear dead. Then once in the cave he was brought round with another drug and received healing from the Essenes before being smuggled away to Egypt where he and Mary spent the rest of their lives. This discussion lasted the whole journey down to Maggie's home. The next day Maggie, Pat and I went to the healing festival and while we were browsing through the marquees I came across a stand that had, among other items, a book. On the front cover was a beautiful painting of a waterfall, a dove and the face of Jesus. I was drawn to it and picked it up to have a look. The lady on the stand watched me and then said that as I was drawn to the book I might like to attend a workshop that the authors of the book were holding in ten minutes' time, which would be all about the book, Jesus and the Essenes.

Maggie and Pat said that they would come with me so we quickly found the tent where it was being held. We crept in and sat down in the back row, with me sitting between them. I was fascinated by what the authors were saying as a lot of it was similar to the discussion Pat and I had had in the car the day before. During the workshop we were taken on a guided meditation. In it I could see an aerial view of a desert with lots of rocky places and some caves in the bigger rocks. I saw hundreds of people sitting on the ground on a plateau, and on a slightly raised area I saw Jesus in a white robe, surrounded by his disciples. I realised that he was giving one of his sermons. We were then called back from the meditation and I found myself sobbing uncontrollably. It had felt so emotional and I knew that I was really there. Maggie and Pat didn't seem so affected by the meditation but I just couldn't stop sobbing, which worried them. I then heard sobbing coming from the end of our row, and as I looked up I saw a man with his head in his hands, crying too. The lady with him was looking very concerned and stroking his back to console him. As I looked at him he lifted his head and looked straight at me, and gave a slight nod of his head in recognition. He knew that we had both been there. The authors looked at us and said that the Essenes were gathering again at this time in our history, that they have reincarnated in our time. One of them took our names and addresses and asked if we would be willing to be regressed. I said no, I felt too emotional at the time. This was a few years ago now, but every year I receive an invitation to the Essene Gathering and maybe one year I shall go.

During meditation in another circle, I did the same thing of sitting in a garden waiting for my guide to come. This time, when I opened my eyes I had to continue looking upwards because the figure in front of me was extremely tall. He was slim in build and had a remarkable sharp-boned face and skin that looked silvery-blue. He was wearing a silver cloak that fell from a short collar at the neck to the floor. I felt an instant recognition of this being, and the love that poured between us had me in tears of happiness. He held out his thin, bony hand and I took it and stood next to him. He put one arm around my shoulders which made his long cloak drape around me and shimmer like silver.

In my mind I asked him his name and he answered, "Simeon." The scene changed and although we were still standing together with his arm around me we were now standing on top of a planet, so high up that I could see the curve of the horizon. Simeon lifted up his other arm and pointed out into space. He was pointing at a little blue and green 'ball' which I suddenly realised was the Earth. He was showing me that this was where I was going. I looked in awe at this beautiful planet and felt so proud that I had been chosen to go there. That was a meditation I was reluctant to come back from.

Around this time I was told by someone about the Chalice Well Gardens in Glastonbury and the wonderful meditation areas there. I had never been to Glastonbury at that time and wondered if I would ever get the chance; then a few months later my husband and I had the opportunity to go to Somerset with his brother and sister-in-law, so we chose a holiday park not far from Glastonbury.

My parents looked after the girls, so we set off for our grown-ups long weekend.

The four of us visited lots of interesting places including Cheddar Gorge, where we had the exciting experience of seeing a stag on the cliff side of the gorge, surveying all before him in the early mist. On our last day we decided to go to Glastonbury before setting off for home. The others wanted to explore the town but I persuaded my husband to look for the Chalice Well Gardens. As we walked up to the small ticket booth I could feel the energy already changing around me. My husband bought our entry tickets and the elderly lady serving him was chatting away as she gave him his change, but he noticed it wasn't correct. She apologised profusely and went to get some more change out of the till, at which point I noticed that two of her fingers were crooked and stiff, making it difficult for her to pick up the change. Then as she handed it to my husband she started to tell us all about her medical problems: she had a bad back that had already been operated on twice and she was now in pain again and waiting for another operation. We finally walked away to view the gardens and I wondered if she told everyone who bought a ticket the same thing.

We came to the beautiful meditation area and, to my surprise, in amongst some shrubs and bushes was a marble angel bench. So of course that's where we had to sit. It was very quiet being a weekday so not many people were around. I closed my eyes and started to daydream. I felt the warm sun shining down on me and could see the golden sunlight shining through my eyelids. I could hear the rustling of the bushes as some small animal hurried through and I could hear the birds singing. As I daydreamed I thought about a shop that had become vacant in my home town. It was on the corner of a small parade with its own car park at the front. This shop had windows on two sides and I was thinking of what I could do with it. My hobby is glass painting, turning unwanted glass items into something useable. I pictured my painted glass on display in one of the windows, catching the light and sending colour all over the shop.

There was a room at the back of this shop that I thought I could perhaps turn into my healing room, so that I could offer Reiki as well as my painted glass. I then thought about what else I could sell in the shop and imagined crystals on shelves, books on spiritual items, angel cards, Tarot cards... As soon as I thought this, a stern male voice in my head said, "No! You will not touch the Tarot, you will only deal with what you know." I was astonished – where had that voice come from? I apologised in my mind and my thoughts drifted back to the lady in the booth. Maybe she wasn't aware how much she had told us about her medical problems. Maybe I should give her some Reiki... Once again that stern male voice in my head said loudly, "You may offer to give her healing, you cannot just give it. She has free will." I felt humbled so again I apologised. Then I started to wonder what the time was and slowly opened my eyes. To my surprise, the sky was overcast and it was a bit chilly so I asked my husband what had happened to the sun. He looked at me as if I were mad and declared that it had been overcast the whole time I had been 'away'. It had been spiritual energy flowing over me, not the sun.

I still felt strongly that I had to ask this lady if she would like some healing but my husband was getting restless. He felt that the lady would be offended, and he also wanted to get back to his brother's car. I asked him to wait just a little longer while I went to ask the lady, so he agreed and walked off to another part of the gardens. I plucked up courage and tapped on the glass window of the booth. She smiled at me kindly and I said, "Please don't be offended but I am a Reiki healer and would like to offer you some Reiki. If you don't want it then please don't be angry." She smiled at me and said, "Come in dear, come in. You are most welcome." It wasn't until I went into the booth that I saw she was propped up on cushions and had a walking stick tucked down the side. I stood behind her while explaining how I would channel the energy. I then placed my hands lightly on her shoulders and felt the Reiki flowing through me, into my hands and then into her. We chatted quietly while this continued. She told me that she was a retired nursing Sister and had seen wonderful things in her career. Apparently she had clearly seen angels around the beds of those who were dying, and watched their souls leave when their departed loved ones came for them.

She carried on selling entry tickets to people while the Reiki was flowing. To anyone looking in it looked like we were friends having a chat in a small space. After about twenty minutes the Reiki started to slow down and then stop, so it was time for me to go. I asked her if she would like me to send her distant Reiki and she said she would, so we exchanged addresses and then it was time for me to get going. When I found my husband he said, "About time too!" and we raced off to meet up with the others. That lady and I continued to write to each other over the next five months and she would give me progress reports on how she was feeling after I sent Reiki to her. Each time she wrote to me she would send a little gift, bless her. The last I heard from her was a brilliant letter: she told me that her back condition had improved so much that she didn't need the operation any more. Then the best bit was when she wrote that she had thrown away her stick as she could walk very well now without it. A lovely lady, and a lovely ending to our time of being linked.

When the girls were young I always found that by 2 p.m. my energy levels would dip really low and that I needed to have a power nap to re-charge before collecting them from school. I would curl up in the armchair and nod off, slightly concerned that I wouldn't wake up at 2.45 in time to collect them. Then one day while I was napping I heard that stern male voice again, saying "Christine, Christine!" I woke up with a jolt and saw that it was exactly 2.45. From then on, every time I had an afternoon nap I was woken by the same stern voice calling my name.

On another occasion, I was driving home from work one evening in October. As I got to my town, the level crossing barriers were down at the railway station. Mine was the fifth car in the queue. I turned off the engine but as the lights were still on the warning sound was driving me mad, so I switched everything off. Sitting in the dark waiting for the train to come through, I idly looked around to see what was going on around me. There is a public footpath that goes over the railway and connects the platforms, and I noticed a young man in his late twenties moving along the bridge. He was unsteadily shuffling one step at a time and as I watched he kept patting his body in different places as if he didn't know where it began or ended. It crossed my mind that there was something very strange about him but I glanced away to see if the train was coming so that I could start the engine.

At that moment, the stern voice said very urgently, "Lock the car doors." I wondered why - although dark it was only 9 o'clock, there were plenty of people about and the train would be here soon. As I thought this the voice shouted at me, "Lock the car doors NOW!" This made me jump, and just as I touched the central locking button I looked up and saw the strange young man's face pressed right up against the window on my side, with the most evil, sickly grin on his face as he tried to open the car door. Our eyes met for a brief second and I could feel the evil energy in him. He tried the door handle again but when he realised he couldn't get it open he suddenly turned and lurched off down the road into the night.

My poor heart was racing and I felt the shock surge through me. The barriers came back up and I shakily drove the rest of the way home. My husband could see that I was shaken and was very concerned about what had happened. I told him there were four other cars in front of mine and about eight behind me - so why did the young man pick on my car? Neither of us could understand it; perhaps he had been on drugs, which would account for his strange behaviour and movements.

Although I never actually saw my guide with the stern voice, other people with psychic abilities could. I had a client whose sister could see energy but I wasn't aware of it when I first visited them. One day I was chatting with her and suddenly she started looking up high above my head. She asked me who the very tall, stern-looking man was behind me. I told her that it sounded possibly like my guide and said that I had heard his voice, mostly telling me off. She carried on looking up and told me that I'd made him smile when I said that. She then nodded her head and said that although he was strict with me he loved me dearly. I thanked her for the message, and then she asked, "Who is the jolly Japanese man with you, wearing a green silk robe with golden dragons?" I said that sounded like a Reiki guide, which reminded me that I had better get on and see her sister. At this she burst out laughing and told me that my stern guide had said, "Good, it's about time. You came here to work, not talk."

The medium who had run the circle in Essex wanted to travel down to me because she was ready to do the Level II Reiki course, so we arranged it for the following month. It was lovely to see her, and on the first morning of her attunement she looked around my healing room and told me that the room was full of spirits and angels. It made me very happy that the energy in the room had brought them to me. Just as I was about to start, she described to me an oriental gentleman in a brown robe who was standing in front of us. He had a young boy with him, the gentleman's apprentice. She told me that they were there to honour what I was about to do, and then she exclaimed, "Oh Chris, they're bowing to you", which made me feel quite emotional.

CHAPTER SEVEN

A Family Affair

My elder daughter was quite receptive to spirit energy and when she was seventeen she showed an interest in the Wiccan traditions. I happened to mention this one day to the medium who ran the circle I attended in Essex; to my surprise she told me she was a Wiccan priestess and that if my daughter had 'the gift' then she would be happy to train her in the Wiccan way. My daughter seemed interested but a little shy about meeting the medium so we arranged to meet all together for lunch the following week.

We set off in plenty of time but many things slowed us down. First of all it was a learner driver, then a tractor on the country road, then a lorry. Then there were some temporary traffic lights due to road works where the medium lived. I couldn't believe how slow our journey had been and we were at least half an hour late by the time we arrived. I apologised profusely to our hostess for being so late; she laughed and said not to worry as she had cast a spell to delay us because she had forgotten something from the supermarket that she needed to get for lunch! That was one of many times the efficiency of spells was shown to me.

The three of us went into the lounge and the medium asked us to take a seat while she put the kettle on for a cup of tea. A few minutes later she was back, holding a jar of water. She handed this to my daughter and asked her what kind of water it was. My daughter looked over to me in panic but I told her to take a deep breath, relax, and say the first thing that came into her mind. She blurted out "Moon water." The medium was impressed and asked whether it was a waxing or a waning moon. My daughter answered straight away, "Waning"; the medium smiled, told us that my daughter had the gift and then went to make the tea.

During lunch they talked about training and it was decided that as my daughter would be going to university soon, they would leave the training until she was ready. Everyone has free will. In fact, after three years at university my daughter decided to stay in the area and lead a 'normal' life, and she is now a proud mum herself. She and her husband gave me a beautiful grand-daughter last year. I didn't think it was possible to love a baby who isn't your own so much. I look forward to watching her grow and to see if she has inherited any of her grandmother's and mum's 'spooky' side.

My younger daughter was seven years old when I took my Reiki Level I and II qualifications. She was fascinated to feel the energy coming through my hands when I gave her Reiki for any bumps or bruises. She started asking if she could learn Reiki too but I kept telling her she was too young – she badgered me for a whole year and my answer was always the same.

When she was about eight we took her along with us to a London Mind Body and Spirit exhibition. I loved attending this event every year and it always felt as if I had 'come home'. The scent of burning incense would waft up the corridor before you even entered the main hall. As the three of us walked around the exhibitors' stands, psychics and spiritual people came up to pat her on the head and tell us that she was 'an old soul'. I was aware vaguely of what they meant. When she was about eighteen months old she would get very distressed and cry, saying that she wanted to "go home". This used to really worry me because she was so determined that I honestly feared that she would do something to herself to get her back. She had been born with the memory of where she had come from...

At such a tender age I explained to her that she had chosen to be with her Mummy and Daddy, that we loved her very much and wanted her to stay with us. I then said I didn't think that God would be very happy if she went home before she was meant to. At this she just looked me straight in the eye and I knew she had understood – at eighteen months of age. So it was no surprise to have these people come up and tell us what a special child she was.

Her favourite treat at these events was frozen yoghurt so she went off with her dad to buy some. I walked a little further on and to my surprise I saw my Reiki Master at a stand, giving out leaflets and talking to people, while some of his students were giving Reiki 'tasters' to the public. I went over to say hello and we had a Reiki hug and chatted about what we had been doing since the training weekend. While this was going on my daughter had wandered back to me with her frozen yoghurt and stood there, listening to our conversation. My Reiki Master kept glancing in her direction and in the end asked if she belonged to me. I told him that she was my daughter. He smiled at her, then looked at me and said, "You know she's a special one, don't you?" I said I did, and so did all the psychics we had passed on our way down the aisles. Then I told him that she'd been badgering me for a year to learn Reiki but I had kept telling her she was too young. He looked at me thoughtfully, then said that six months ago he would have totally agreed with me, but he'd had so many parents telling him that their children were demanding to learn Reiki that he'd asked his guides for advice and had been told that the children were ready. He looked down at my daughter, smiled and said, "She's ready." So two weeks later we were back in Kent for her to take her children's Reiki Level I course.

At the end of the day the children - there were four of them, and one had even flown in from Germany with his mum just to do the course - were attuned to the Reiki energy individually by my Reiki Master, while his partner channelled the information of what she sensed for each child. I was standing in the doorway of the room watching, and the pure look of bliss on my daughter's face made me feel quite emotional. The German mum was standing next to me and whispered, "Your daughter is an angel." I smiled and whispered back, "You haven't seen her at home having a strop!" She smiled but shook her head and said, "No, your daughter IS an angel... I can see her energy."

When the attunements were finished and it was time to go home with all their silver and purple balloons and coloured-in pictures, my Reiki Master came over to me, grinned and said, "Your daughter's hand went up with the answer to every question I asked them – I could tell she was yours!" His partner gave me what she had channelled for my daughter. I read it in the car on the way home while my husband drove and talked to her about her how her day had been and how she was feeling. I was amazed by what I was reading. 'This is a blessed child who has drunk from the holy chalice. Angels surround her and she will travel the world bringing healing wherever she goes.' I have kept this sheet of paper safe as it is so special.

She would later come with me to Reiki Shares (where healers of all levels come together to give healing to each other). Bless her, she was always the youngest there, though her energy was just as strong as the adults'.

One evening my husband and I were attending a Parents' Evening at her school; her teacher started to laugh and said that our daughter had caused a lot of amusement in the Staff Room. The class had been asked to draw a picture, and the normal things to draw at their age were trees, houses or a dog. Our daughter had drawn a woman meditating! Around this time, some of the other mums at the school gate were asking me if I knew that my daughter and their child talked to their guardian angels at break time... I said that I wasn't aware and asked if there was a problem – they hastily said "No" and walked away.

My daughter had her Reiki attunement when she was in the junior school but she was never bullied or made to feel different. The teachers were quite used to her helping out others who had hurt themselves. I was very touched one day when her young teacher asked me if we could help her mother who'd been diagnosed with breast cancer. I said that we could try but there were no guarantees or promises. My daughter and I sent Reiki to the lady for seven months but then sadly she passed away. However, the teacher thanked us for helping her because she hadn't been in the pain that the doctors had predicted, and she died peacefully at home in her own bed with her family around her.

Another time I was at the school Sports Day. One of my daughter's friends was running in the relay when unfortunately she tripped and went skidding on her knees across the grass. One of the teachers rushed over to the crying child, then looked around and called out for my daughter because her 'magic hands' were needed! I was so proud that this young child had brought teachers and friends with her on her spiritual journey.

One last event stays in my mind. One of her favourite teachers had been promoted to Head Teacher and she was so happy for him. But one day she came home quite sad and told me that this man was now going to another school. As the date got nearer, she asked me if she could give him the present of a Reiki session with me. I agreed and gave her one of my business cards so he would know how to contact me, and she wrote a message on the back of it. However, on the day of his leaving she came home quite indignant. It transpired that he had taken assembly for the last time and the theme was 'gifts'. He'd said that not all great gifts were big ones, and then to her embarrassment he had taken my business card from his wallet and told the whole school that she'd given it to him. He said that although it was small it was the thought behind it that had made it one of the best presents he had ever had. At this the whole school had turned around to look at her.

This teacher never did contact me, though, yet I think it was the thoughtfulness of a ten year old that had been the real gift.

When she was fourteen, she felt ready to take Level II. Although I was a Reiki Master myself by then, I felt it would be better for her to have an energy that was outside the family. My 'soul sister' Pat, whom I had met through Reiki, was also a Reiki Master and she was more than happy to have my daughter on her next course. It turned out to be a very special time for both of them. My daughter met her guides and Pat was amazed by what she had seen and been told about my daughter from her own guides during the attunement. She was also told that the guides were stepping back to allow her a normal life until she was ready to work with them again. I think that time will come soon.

Although I never had much interest in computers, when they first became available to the public my husband loved them. He was fascinated by all the technology and predicted that everyone would have one in the house in the not-too-distant future. It used to irritate me when he spent hours on them, writing programs for games and building computers from bits and pieces of old ones. He was right, though - nearly thirty years on from his prediction nearly everyone has a computer in their home.

After quite a few attempts of trying to get me interested, I finally relented and he showed me how to go online and so on. We only had one computer then and we shared an email address, but weird things would happen whenever I used it. Things wouldn't work properly, or the screen would freeze, which really frustrated him when he went to use it after me. One day a friend came over to visit and asked if I had seen the email she'd sent me. I hadn't, so my husband checked the computer and opened up the email. The message was a joke and as I read it my friend told me that I had to click the mouse to get the punch line. Now, my husband was wary about me touching his computer but my friend told him not to be so mean, so he begrudgingly let me click the mouse – and of course it froze the screen. My friend gasped as my husband said, "I knew this would happen!", then beat a hasty retreat. The screen stayed frozen for the next three hours. Because of this, my husband decided to build my own computer so I would no longer need to use his. But things would regularly happen on my one and I've lost count of how many times I called him to see why it was doing something it shouldn't. He would roll his eyes and say, "I have no idea. That should be impossible in theory." One day I put my hands behind my head and then called him to see what was happening on the screen; to his astonishment the cursor was moving around without me touching the mouse...

It became a bit of a family joke, the effect I had on computers, but it soon became known outside the family too. When I was working as a Reiki therapist for the council, I sometimes had to come down to the main Reception area so that the receptionists could ring someone if they were late for an appointment. The two receptionists sat at their computers but whenever I stood near them the machines wouldn't work. It became a joke there, too, that I had to stand away from the desk before the computers would work properly.

When I moved down to the south-west I applied for a job on the Staff Bank at the local hospital. At my interview I thought I'd better be honest and tell them that I had a problem with computers. The interviewer gave me a strange look but wrote it down on my application sheet. A month later I had a call to say that a job was available for a few days, which I accepted gratefully. But on the day I was ushered into the office of a very harassed manager who promptly sat me down in front of a computer and told me to merge the two lists that were there, to send emails and to type up and save the agenda for the following day's meeting. I took a deep breath and told her I was happy to do all that, but that it may not go according to plan. She glared at me as if I were mad and stomped off to her desk. Luckily she was in the same room so could see everything I was doing. At lunch time she came over to see how I was getting on and whether I had finished. We found that the merged list had separated itself again, we couldn't find the agenda for love nor money on the computer, and none of the eighty-nine emails ever reached their destination (and are probably still floating around in the ether today). I was put on paper duties for the rest of the few days I was there and then they let me go. I went over to the Staff Bank office and told them what had happened. The manager couldn't believe her ears, although the note was still on my file. She then laughed and picked up the 'phone to find me another job. She spoke to someone in the X-ray department and I heard her say, "She can't use computers" to which I indignantly replied, "I can use computers, but they just don't want to work for me." The manager came off the 'phone laughing. It turned out that all the X-rays were now stored digitally and it was thought that I was too dangerous to be around them. That's how I ended up on paper duties in Pathology Reception for the next four years.

During a conversation with my financial advisor, I had mentioned my effect on computers but he just raised his eyebrows and said nothing. We didn't get everything done at that meeting so we arranged to meet on another day at his office in town. The following week I sat in the waiting area. After a few minutes the advisor appeared and asked me to follow him. As we walked down the corridor to his office he kept turning his head to look at me, which I thought was rather strange, and when he opened his office door I asked him if there was anything wrong. He rushed over to his laptop, protectively pulling it towards him as I sat down opposite. He looked at me for a long time and then said that after our last meeting - where he admitted he had thought I was slightly bonkers for telling him about my effect on computers - his laptop had frozen for two hours after I'd left, which had made it very difficult for him to work the rest of the afternoon because he couldn't get his clients' information up on the screen. I laughed and told him that those who doubted me found out the hard way!

I now know it's 'a family thing'. My elder daughter took a computer course while at college and every week the IT man had to come and sort out the computer she was using. She tried using different computers each week but still the screens would freeze or she would have trouble accessing information. She was the only one he had to come out to every week.

My dad is in his seventies. Eventually he bought a laptop so he could keep in touch with his family by email and Skype calls. He was so excited about getting onto the Internet but now he's very disappointed. The laptop keeps freezing or it won't accept his password, and so on. When he told me this I suddenly realised it must be in the genes – it had taken this long to find out that I got this 'gift' from him and have passed it on to my elder daughter. Luckily my younger daughter takes after her dad and is a whiz kid on computers and often sorts out my problems. Even to this day, Maggie shakes her head when I show her what my computer is doing; she has a go at fixing it but has trouble understanding why it does what it does. I recently set up a business website with the help of a wonderful IT man but it was fraught with things not going according to plan. Even when he took over control remotely he had trouble sorting things out.

I have also been lucky to be a guest on the local BBC radio station, but even there I have a reputation. One day we went off air for over a minute, which is a long time in the radio world. The BBC also have a mobile studio for when they're out and about, but the man who looked after it would look panic-stricken if he saw me approaching 'his baby'. It will be interesting to see if this gene gets passed down to any future grandchildren.

CHAPTER EIGHT

Soul Sisters

I have already mentioned how I met Maggie. Well, we've been blessed with another 'soul sister' in Pat whom we met a few years after we had taken our Reiki I and II qualifications. Our Reiki Master had asked Maggie and me to help out on a stand at a local Mind Body and Spirit exhibition. We looked forward to seeing each other and meeting other Reiki healers, and there was a lady we hadn't seen before but whose energy felt wonderful. We had the same sense of humour and would bounce off each other when talking to the public who stopped to ask questions. When the day came to an end, one of the men working on the stand suggested we all got fish and chips for supper at his home and wind down after such a busy day. In the end there were twelve of us there, including Maggie, Pat and me.

We all sat around a large dining table and the conversation just flowed. The energy in the room was fantastic. Maggie and I talked with Pat most of the evening and enjoyed her company even more. Before we left, our host informed us that he was having a party to celebrate his fiftieth birthday and he invited us all. So the following week I went along with my husband and younger daughter. Maggie couldn't make it but I was very happy to see that Pat was there. I introduced her to my family and I think we spent most of the evening talking. Before we left, our host told us that he was going to hold a Reiki Share once a month at his house and asked if we would like to come along. Pat and I both said we would.

When we next met up, Pat confessed to me that normally she never went back to people's homes after an exhibition and didn't know why she had that day. She also confessed that she'd never been to a party on her own so had surprised herself by turning up at the birthday bash. We agreed that it was meant to happen so that we would meet. Over the years our friendship grew and I felt so blessed to have two such wonderful sisters. I never had a real one, being the eldest of four with three younger brothers. Every year the three of us would attend Mind Body and Spirit exhibitions, not to work but to try out other therapies and buy crystals.

One year our Reiki Share group felt a 'pull' to visit the standing stones at Avebury, Wiltshire. Seven of us went for the weekend, including Maggie, Pat and me. We didn't know what we were going to do once we were there but it just felt important that we went. The weather was atrocious, torrential downpours of rain keeping the tourists at bay. We had travelled in three cars and I was in Maggie's. She asked me if I knew what we were to do with the standing stones, and as she said it an image flashed into my mind of the seven of us linking hands around the 'male' stone in the centre of a circle of sentinel 'female' stones. I mentioned this to Maggie and she agreed. All three cars met up in the car park and as the others got out they said that they'd also been shown us all linking hands around the stone.

The rain continued to pelt down as we trudged through the field to get to the single male stone set in the middle of it. No-one else was around (sensible people) as we slipped about in the mud. We stood facing the stone and as we linked hands a flock of crows came straight at us from a group of trees in the field. They swooped over us and then formed the shape of an arrow before swooping over us again and then flying off into the distance. This was a bit unsettling and we weren't sure what it signified.

Unknown to us, one of the ladies had brought her flute with her and she felt the need to play it. It was very surreal standing in a muddy field, hands linked together, the rain pouring down on us and listening to the haunting sound of the flute. After a moment of quiet when she finished I had another flash in my mind of what we were to do next; but I hate being seen as a leader so I kept quiet, waiting to see if anyone else had also seen it. I had been shown us walking seven steps to the left and then seven steps to the right. One man said he had been told to move to the left so I knew I'd been shown the same thing. So in the rain and mud we slipped seven steps to the left and then seven steps to the right. To me, it felt as if we were 'unscrewing' something. We then closed our eyes and sent energy to the male stone. To my amazement, I saw a white light rise up from the top of the stone and splash over all of us. I was then shown that we had to spread this white light on the sentinel female stones around us. Pat could also see the infinity symbol and one man had seen a door open with steps leading down under the stone.

After we shared what we had seen, we spread out to take the light to the other stones. As I was walking towards my third stone, Maggie walked past me. The rain had stopped by now so she didn't have the hood up on her coat. I called her name but she just walked straight past me, her face pale and her eyes large and looking glazed. I called her name again but she still didn't look at me. I became concerned because she was heading towards the road that runs through this area, but Pat said she would keep an eye on her. We watched as Maggie mumbled something while making strange hand movements over the standing stones in front of her. Pat walked slowly up to her and when she got near, without looking, Maggie held her hand out to her. Pat took it and to our surprise the two of them walked slowly away, hand in hand, until they were by the stones at the furthest edge of the field. We watched as they made strange hand passes over the stones there and then slowly walked back to us, hand in hand. When they reached us they started to blink their eyes and look confused. The colour was coming back into their faces and they looked at each other in bewilderment at what had just happened.

Maggie said that as she started to spread the white light on the stones she began to feel strange. She then saw a lot of symbols scrolling down in front of her eyes and it felt as though she was being programmed with what she had to say and the hand movements she was to make. She didn't recognise the language that she was mumbling and her hands had spontaneously started to move. She wasn't aware of us being near her and only registered that Pat was near, which is why she held her hand out to her.

Pat was just as confused. She told us she was aware of moving towards Maggie to see if she was all right, and as soon as Maggie held out her hand she could also see strange symbols scrolling down in front of her eyes and her hands also spontaneously started to move across the stones. When they'd finished, they walked hand in hand down an avenue of stones that the rest of us couldn't see because they were no longer there. They saw themselves wearing white robes with green garlands on their heads, looking young. It was an amazing end to an amazing day. We all felt that something very special had happened and that we'd been called to be a part of it.

Another time, the three of us went for a healing event near to where Maggie and I live. Pat drove down from Essex to join us for a long weekend. The three of us decided to book a session with a young psychic surgeon we met there. For some reason Maggie and I were taken off site to the healing sanctuary of the man who had organised the weekend, while Pat was seen at the exhibition marquee. Maggie went in first to see one of the psychic surgeon's students and about ten minutes into her session I heard a startled voice and then Maggie laughing. When she came out she told me excitedly that she had levitated off the couch, much to the shock of the lady treating her! Maggie had been enjoying the treatment and feeling very relaxed when she suddenly realised she was about an inch off the couch. As soon as she realised this she suddenly fell back onto it. Maggie thought it was hysterical which is why I heard her laughing. We couldn't wait to meet up with Pat again and tell her what had happened. My own session was straightforward, which was a big relief to the healer.

Later in the day Pat had a wax reading done with one of the exhibitors. She came back full of praise for this man and how accurate he had been so Maggie and I decided to book him for the following day. Maggie's reading was the one before mine so, to give her privacy, I went to watch a performance on the stage. As I checked my watch to see if it was time to head back, I saw Pat making her way through the marquee to meet us at the wax reading stand. When I got there Pat was sitting on the only spare chair next to Maggie, so I stood behind them placing my hands on the backs of their chairs and leaning forward. The man looked up and exclaimed, "Oh my God. I have the Trinity in front of me!" He seemed overwhelmed and told us that although we had our own individual energy, together we were powerful. He asked if anything special had happened when the three of us were together and when we told him about Avebury he nearly fell off his chair with excitement. He said there was a 'portal' near the field that we'd been in and he was being told by his guide that the three of us could open it. Through his guide he told us what to do and when to do it. He was so excited and asked if he could come and observe us; but then his face fell because his guide had told him it was for our eyes only. He said it was an honour for him to have 'the Trinity' at his stand; but now his next client was waiting so we said goodbye and left.

We decided it was time to go back to Maggie's, where we were based, and think this through. Over a glass of wine we discussed what had been said. Intuitively we already knew that the energy was more powerful when we were together, because strange things happened. We were curious about the portal and wondered what that was about, so agreed to go back to Avebury at the time he had told us to see what would happen. Once I got home I excitedly told my younger daughter all about it, but she looked horrified so I asked her what was wrong. She asked me not to go, pointing out that we only had this man's word that we would be safe. She said she was scared that something might happen or that we might go through the portal and not be able to get back. Her eyes filled with tears as she said, "Please don't go, Mum. I'm only sixteen and about to take my A Levels. If you disappeared they would take me away in a straightjacket if I told them you'd gone through a portal. Please don't do it, Mum, I couldn't stand the stress."

Seeing her distress, my mother's love overrode my spiritual wish so I promised I wouldn't go. Later I rang Maggie and she was glad that my daughter had been the voice of caution; I rang Pat and she immediately agreed too, so the decision was made not to follow the plan. Although now and again I wonder what would have happened, I have never regretted my decision.

Our times with Pat became more precious when she and her family moved out to Spain to live. She had felt a calling to go there and between them they bought an olive farm up in the Catalonian mountains. The plan was to turn it into a healing retreat. Maggie and I would fly out once a year to see her and she would fly here for the healing weekends.

On one of those years while I was still living in Essex, Pat had flown to Stansted and hired a car to pick me up for the drive to Maggie's. During the four hour drive we had plenty of time to catch up with what had been going on in our lives. We all had a brilliant weekend at a local festival, and for a change the weather was kind to us. Pat decided she wanted to buy a crystal ball at the festival so we set off in search of one and finally found a stand where a lady who was giving Indian head massage had one for sale. This lady had a client in her chair so couldn't come over to us straight away. Pat picked up the crystal ball and looked into it, to see if she could see anything. Maggie also held it and peered into it and then it was my turn. Neither Maggie nor I could see anything but Pat felt a connection with it.

When we were back at Maggie's that evening she made us supper and as it was a nice evening we sat outside to eat. We brought out all the things we had bought that day to show Maggie's husband. Maggie peered into the crystal ball again and this time said she could see a picture forming. She saw a field with cows in it, but her husband was very sceptical and said it was her imagination. Then Pat peered into it she said that she could see a bunch of bananas… I started to laugh because what she was seeing was her own hand holding the ball and the hand and fingers were being distorted because of the curve of the ball. We all ended up laughing hysterically, though I think the wine we were drinking had a lot to do with it!

Sadly, the next day it was time to go home. Maggie's husband put our bags in the boot of the hired car and we hugged each other goodbye. Maggie was planning to have a quiet and restful day after all the excitement of the weekend. Pat had a 'plane to catch that evening and I was looking forward to going home to my husband and daughters. As we were driving on our way to the motorway, I noticed a strange cloud formation in a beautiful blue sky. I pointed it out to Pat and we both agreed it looked like an angel with its wings outstretched. It stayed with us for miles, even when we were on the motorway. Now, when Pat drives she likes just to keep going until she reaches her destination without any stops, but on this occasion she decided to stop for a coffee at a service station. Once parked, we got out to stretch our legs and Pat opened the boot to get out her handbag. I saw her move the cases around and then start to frown. She said she couldn't find the handbag, so I looked under the seats but there were only carrier bags containing the things we had bought over the weekend.

Poor Pat looked quite frantic and realised she must have left her bag with her passport and boarding pass at Maggie's; but I told her not to worry, that Maggie was on her way. I didn't know how I knew this, I just did. The battery had gone flat on my 'phone and Pat's was in the handbag, so I found a public 'phone and rang my home. My younger daughter answered and said that Maggie had already called and told us to wait for her at the service station. We did as we were told and went for a coffee, and within fifteen minutes Maggie walked through the door with Pat's handbag! She told us that she had seen it ten minutes after we left and had tried ringing us but couldn't get an answer, so jumped into her car and asked the angels for help to get us to stop before we were too far away. Pat and I looked at each other and burst out laughing. We told Maggie that we had seen the angel cloud but hadn't realised it was a message… Pat was so relieved to get her bag back and we were both grateful to our soul sister for driving all that way to catch us up.

We all feel very lucky and blessed with the friendship we have. We've supported each other through some very tough times including my cancer journey and the sudden death of my beloved husband at the age of fifty-two. Pat living in Spain has made no difference to our friendship and we still try to meet up a few times a year.

CHAPTER NINE

The Extraordinary (Part 1)

There have been so many other weird and wonderful things that have happened in my life.

When I was in my mid-twenties, sadly I had a very early miscarriage. I wasn't aware that I was pregnant at the time so it came as a shock. I didn't know if we had lost a son or a daughter but for years afterwards I would think about the child and imagine what they would have looked like as they grew older. About twenty years after this sad time, and now a mum to my two daughters, my family went to stay with some friends of ours who lived in the north and had children the same age as ours. My friend had also started on a spiritual path and asked me if I would like to join her in an 'open circle'. I asked her to explain what that was and she told me she had started going to this circle recently and had checked to see if I could come with her. This was before I had started sitting in a circle in Essex so I was intrigued about what went on. The following morning we left our husbands in charge of the children and set off.

It was held in a church hall and in total there were seven of us, plus the medium. The only person I knew there was my friend but the medium was a nice, friendly lady and welcomed me. We started with a meditation on opening up the chakras. I was familiar with this method but was suddenly surprised when the medium referred to a different colour to the one I was expecting. I continued following her guided meditation but it felt weird. We were then 'called back' and she went to each person, asking if everyone was all right. When she got to me, she laughed and said that I had made her doubt herself when I questioned the order she had taken. It was then I realised that she had somehow seen my hesitation. I was stunned – I had only just met this lady but she could see into my meditation. My friend grinned when she saw the look on my face.

The medium then led us on another guided meditation to meet our loved ones in the spiritual world. Guided meditation was new to me but I found that I could see things before the medium told us they were there. For example, she had taken us on a journey to a big country house in its own grounds. I could see the marble pillars outside the front door before she described them to us. Once inside I saw a black and white marble chequered floor with a sweeping staircase to the right of the enormous hall. I so wanted to run up those stairs but we hadn't yet been told that they were there... She then told us that we were free to go anywhere in the house or grounds and that we would meet loved ones there; there was a staircase to the right and that was enough for me, I was off!

I ran up the staircase and walked along a corridor with doors on either side, drawn to a door on the right. As I opened the door I saw that it was painted white and that it was a nursery. There was a white cot with a white mobile hanging over it, a white carpet and white walls. The room had a beautiful large bay window with a seat in it, and sitting there was my maternal grandmother. Sitting next to her was a young man who looked vaguely familiar but I couldn't make out why. They were both dressed in white and stood up to greet me. Not a word was said but their loving and welcoming smiles let me know that I was loved. They beckoned for me to sit between them on the window seat, which I did, and we sat in silence, watching those who had decided to roam the grounds. The sun had started to go down, filling the room with a warm orange glow. Nan and the young man stood up and I knew it was time for me to go, but I was worried as the medium hadn't called us back yet. I hugged them and said goodbye and told them how much I loved them. As I put my hand on the door handle I heard the medium telling us to say our goodbyes to our loved ones and make our way back. I was relieved, as I wasn't sure what I would have done when I left the nursery if she hadn't called us back.

Once we had all returned from the meditation she spoke to us one at a time, asking who we had seen. A few people were quite emotional, talking about their loved ones and the time they had spent with them. When she got to me I told her that I had gone to the nursery and that my maternal grandmother had been there with a young man whom I had thought looked familiar but didn't know why. She smiled at me and told me gently that he was my son, the baby I had lost all those years ago. Then it clicked into place why he looked familiar - he looked like a younger version of my baby brother, a very strong family resemblance.

She told me that his name was Adam (a name I would have chosen if I had a boy) and that she had had the privilege of working with him recently. She said he thought I was ready to meet him now. I felt such a warm glow knowing that my baby was safe. He wanted to meet me and he'd been working with this medium. She then told me that he would be one of my helpers in spirit, when I was on my own spiritual path. This was such a lovely thing to hear.

When we got back I told my husband. He was very sceptical but I have been reliably informed that when my husband died it was his own father and Adam who met him first to welcome him 'home'. One year, I was at circle on my birthday and during the opening meditation I saw Adam in front of me, looking in his thirties. He smiled at me then hugged me as he said, "Happy birthday, Mum." It was so wonderful. I could feel the pressure of his arms around me and it felt very real. I haven't seen him for a while now but I expect he is helping lots of others.

Talking about my Nan reminded me of all the times she gate-crashed the circle in Essex! She would come through most nights, so much so that the medium asked if I could get her to step back and let some of the others through. One evening we had a new lady join us who was very nervous and had lots of self-doubt about her gifts. After the opening meditation, the medium told us that we had brought spirit back with us and it was now time to ask who they were and whether there were any messages. The poor new lady was struggling and said that she couldn't see or feel anyone. The medium told her that there was someone with her, and asked her to use her imagination to describe this person. Immediately she said, "A woman." Then the medium asked her if this woman was tall or short. The lady said that she was short and a large lady for her size, wearing an old-fashioned 'pinny'. My heart jumped – this was sounding like my Nan. When the medium asked her name the lady sat in thought and then started to frown. She said that when she asked the woman her name, she just kept spinning around and it was making her dizzy. I couldn't help but laugh out loud. My Nan's name was Daisy, and this was the nearest she could get the lady to say it!

She was asked if the woman had a message for anyone in the circle. The new lady was again doubtful of what she was seeing, a candle on a birthday cake. I guiltily put up my hand and said that she was right and that I could understand everything she had said: this was my Nan and that she was letting me know that she would be joining in the celebrations for my daughter's eighteenth birthday party the following day. The lady was flabbergasted that she had actually got all the information correct. And it made my mum very happy to know that her own much loved mum was with us at the party the following day.

On another night the medium chose to talk about the different energies there are, including angel energy. She asked if anyone in the circle had experienced it. I shyly nodded and she gave me a big smile as if to say, "I knew you did"; then she explained to the rest of the ladies how angels are with us but cannot help unless asked.

She then led us on a guided meditation to meet our angels and to ask their names. In my meditation I was in an enormous hall that had black and white marble tiles on the floor. In the middle of this vast place there was a tall rock with steps hewn into the side, leading to a crystal throne on the very top. In an instant I was up there, sitting on the crystal. As I looked down I saw dolphins gliding in and out of the marble floor as if it were water. It was beautiful to watch. Then I heard the medium tell us to ask, gently, the name of our angel. She told us that we might hear a name, or our angel may come to sit beside us. In my mind, I asked my angel to let me know their name in any way they wanted and within seconds a huge white feather floated down from the top of the hall. It looked like a feather from an angel's wing. As it floated gently down in front of me, an invisible hand caught it and held it like a quill pen; very gracefully, the name Ariel was written in the air. I suddenly felt quite emotional as I looked at the name hovering in front of me. I thanked my angel Ariel for sharing their name with me and as I watched the letters gradually began to fade away. It was then that the medium called us back from the meditation.

My lovely mum and dad have always supported me on my spiritual path, so it came as no surprise when they told me certain things about themselves. My dad has flashbacks to a previous life. He described how he saw a man standing in a baronial hall next to a large fireplace that had tile edging around it, and he knew that this man was him and that he was lord of the place. Dad also liked to tinker around with cars and fixing them. One day he told me that he could 'see' through his fingertips, which was a great help when he was underneath a car and couldn't see with his eyes where the nuts and bolts were that he needed to work on.

My mum came from a line of Irish Catholics through her father's side. She was one of six children; the first three were brought up as Catholics and the last three as Church of England! Apparently, her mum (my Nan who gate-crashed circle) secretly corresponded with the great spiritual healer of her time, Harry Edwards. My grandfather would have been very angry if he knew, so Nan kept it from him.

Mum told me once that Harry had sent my Nan a pendant, which she had to hide. Mum wished she knew where it was now, as she felt it should be passed on to me as the healer in the family.

Then one day my mother rang me and said that a psychic museum was opening in York, a place where the public could go to test their psychic abilities. She was so excited, but my dad had refused to drive all that way and she didn't want to go on her own. Then she found that all the tickets had been sold out and she was really disappointed. But a few days later I had a letter through the post and inside was an invitation for myself and a guest to go to the museum! At the time I had been a subscriber to an astrology website, and this invitation had come from there out of the blue. I rang my mum and told her I had it, but didn't know who to take as my guest… I was only teasing her. Bless her, she was so excited, and we arranged to go a few weeks later. Dad was relieved that he didn't have to drive her there, and paid for our coach fares and two nights in a B & B.

Mum and I had never been away together since I had married, so it was great to have that quality time with her. We talked the whole way to York. Once we had found our B & B and left our cases there, we decided to find out where we had to go the following day. We walked along a tarmac path that ran alongside the River Ouse. There were some very tall trees lining the path with areas for picnics on the grass between them. As we walked along, arm in arm, we saw a family having a picnic and smiled at them as we walked by. At that moment we all heard a terrific crashing noise, coming from the very top of one of the trees. The noise continued all the way down the tree and then, right in front of mum and me, a squirrel fell out of the tree and landed hard onto the tarmac path. It had fallen from the very top of the tall tree and at great speed. I'm not a lover of squirrels, but this one looked so damaged lying on the path twitching, with its legs twisted beneath it. I couldn't bear to watch it suffer so dropped my bag onto the path and knelt down beside the battered squirrel. At this point the family who had been picnicking rushed over and a man warned me not to touch an injured animal. I told him I wasn't planning on doing so, then held my hands over the squirrel and felt the Reiki begin to flow. In my head I just kept saying, "Please don't let it suffer." To everyone's amazement, the squirrel stopped twitching, slowly sat up, looked around at us as if in a daze and then scampered off down the path and ran up another tree. The man couldn't believe his eyes, looked at me and said, "That animal was dying. What did you do?" As I stood back up my mum said to him, "My daughter's a healer – she does humans too!" at which I grabbed my bag and her arm and quickly steered her away. Bless her, she was so proud and excited by what had happened, while I felt quite humble that this wonderful energy wanted to work through me.

That night, back at our room, I showed her how to build an energy ball between her hands. She was amazed when she could feel the energy pulsing. I knew my mum had psychic gifts of her own, which I think were passed down from her mother and then to me, but her generation would have frowned on her if she had tried to develop them.

The next day at the psychic museum mum was amazing. Each room and each floor of the building had different types of psychic tests and she scored highly on all of them. The room I remember most was one that had an enormous brass bowl with handles in the shape of dragons on either side. This bowl was filled with water and the museum guide knelt down next to it and started gently to rub the dragon handles. As we watched, the water started to ripple and then a little spout developed in the middle. We all had a go, some couldn't get anything to happen at all, but when it was mum's turn within minutes she had produced a beautiful fountain in the middle of the bowl. Even the museum guide was impressed.

Talking of water, I am a great fan of Dr Masaru Emoto. He is a man who is passionate about water and its memory and healing powers. I read his first book Messages from Water and it fascinated me. There were beautiful photographs of water that had been polluted and then had healing sent to it, with photographs of the water once healed. He had developed a system where water was frozen, then had slivers sliced off and photographed under a lens in a freezer. These images showed the crystal formation of the water molecules. Then either prayers were chanted at the polluted water or loving words taped to the container it was in. It was then frozen and photographed again under the microscope. The difference between the pictures taken before and afterwards was amazing.

One day I read in one of my magazines that Dr Emoto was coming to London to give a talk about his work and to raise money to build a new temple in Tibet (the Chinese government had torn down a lot of temples when they took over). I mentioned this to one of my Reiki students, who said she would like to go along too. We were quite excited on the day as we travelled up by train to London. Our last train was delayed and I was pacing up and down the platform in frustration, because when I had booked the tickets over the 'phone I had been told that if we arrived late we would not be admitted. I kept checking my watch and knew that we would now be late and possibly not be able to get in. Finally the train arrived and once we got to our station we had to run to the venue, another fifteen minutes away. As we came panting up the steps I was desperate for the bathroom, but the nice lady on the door took pity on us and let us in, telling us not to worry as there had been some sort of electrical fault and the talk had been delayed. We finally made our way to our seats, worried that the talk had now started, but to our relief it hadn't and it wasn't until we had sat down and made ourselves comfortable that the electrical fault was fixed. I sent up a silent thank you to the angels for the delay. Dr Emoto's talk was fascinating and at the end of it he signed my copy of his first book. Since then he has written others with some even more amazing photographs.

CHAPTER TEN

Intuition

One day I came across an advertisement of a property for sale in Cornwall. I felt a strong pull towards this and felt very excited. The Reiki Share group I belonged to had one night discussed the idea of opening a healing retreat, but I thought we were just dreaming about it. I looked at the advertisement again - there was a website address, a telephone number and a man's name but no mention of the price. I asked my husband to look at the website and we both watched as photographs of the property came up on the screen. My excitement grew but my husband was concerned that there was still no mention of the price. He thought that if we had to ask the price then we probably wouldn't be able to afford it.

I decided to take a chance and rang the telephone number. The answerphone was on so I just left my number and said I was calling in regard to the property. I was buzzing with excitement but I didn't know why, as I felt that this was just a dream of the Share group. Half an hour later the 'phone rang and a man's voice said, "Hello Chris, it's Tim."[4] It was the owner of the property. It wasn't until later that it suddenly struck me - how did he know my name when I had only given my number when I left the message? I told him that we were a Reiki Share group and had been thinking of opening a healing retreat. He told me that the place was already hosting healing weekends and spiritual work-shops, and that it was booked for the next year, which he had promised to honour.

This was good news as it meant there would be an income while we decided what to do with the place. He also told me the price and I said that obviously I would have to discuss this with the group and would get back to him. Luckily it was Reiki Share the following evening and I told them about the property, that I'd spoken to the owner and then told them the price, expecting them to say "Don't be ridiculous."

But they didn't. Everyone started to get excited and I had for-gotten that among the group were a financial advisor and a bank manager. They started working on how we could raise the money and it was decided that the group would go to view the property and see if it was suitable.

I came home feeling a bit dazed. This was all happening very quickly and it felt as if everyone was looking to me to make the decisions. I rang Tim and arranged for us to view his property the following weekend. Four of us set off for Cornwall in the very early hours of the next Friday morning. Two of the group wanted to stop on the way at another place that they knew was interesting. It was a lovely old house in a busy town, and in each of its large rooms there were different things to try. It was here that I experienced sitting under a pyramid frame to feel the energy for the first time.

We went on to stay overnight at a B & B, ready for our view-ing the following day. The locals had told us how long it would take to reach our destination and suggested that we left no later than 10 a.m. to reach the place by midday, the time we had

---

4   Not his real name.

arranged to meet. Unfortunately it took longer to get four people up, washed, dressed and breakfasted than we had planned and so we were running quite late. I was concerned because Tim was staying at his girlfriend's which was forty miles from the property, a long way for him to come and for us not to be there.

The weather was terrible, torrential rain and windy, so we 'Reikied' the road ahead and the weather, and before we knew it we were arriving at our destination on time with the sun coming out. As we drove down the bumpy lane to the property everything seemed to go quiet. No birds singing, no sound of cars. We were right off the beaten track. The property came into sight and a man was waiting there, standing beside a car.

The place was unique. There was a six-bedroom house that had a conservatory built around a vine. There was a grass tennis court in the grounds, which also had a tepee, an original gypsy caravan and a two-bedroom cottage. A stream also ran through the grounds. We all stood in the kitchen to talk about the property and the price. I thought it strange that although the financial people were asking the questions, the owner only looked at me as he answered. There was a strange look in his eyes as he held my gaze. He told us that there were four definite offers and seven 'bubbling' at the moment, but he was more interested in whom it went to. It had to be the right person.

He said that you could plant anything in the soil and it would grow, even if it wasn't meant to, and confessed that he'd become so obsessed with the land that his marriage had broken up; again, all this was said while looking directly at me. I felt that this was getting a bit too weird so I and another girl in the group left the kitchen to have another wander around the house, leaving the financial discussions to the experts. We came across a bookshelf in the inner hallway that had quite a few books on it, including a few that I had read, and to our surprise there were some copies of a book that Tim had written about the property. My friend and I took one each, went back to the kitchen and bought them from Tim asking if he would sign them for us. He did so and then I felt it was time to leave.

He led us outside and, as we walked around the side of the house, one of the group sensed that there was a hollow space under the earth where we were standing. Tim laughed and was impressed that this had been picked up. He told us it was a Fogou, an ancient underground space that had been there for at least a thousand years. He asked if we would like to see it and the rest of the group agreed, but the girl who bought the book and I decided we didn't want to, so we stood at the mouth of the entrance and waited for the others to come back.

While we waited for them to return, we both felt uneasy. We were standing next to an old tree whose branches hung out over the Fogou. When we looked closer we saw things fluttering amongst the branches and realised they were offerings tied on with ribbons. There was something slightly sinister about it and just at that moment a flock of crows started to dive-bomb us, screeching the whole time. The girl and I had to duck into the entrance of the Fogou to get out of the way, and we were very relieved when we heard the voices of the others returning along the passageway.

Tim walked us to our cars and shook hands with everyone but held mine a fraction longer than necessary, looking straight into my eyes. He said that he hoped to see me soon but I just smiled, said goodbye and jumped into the car. We drove to Penzance to have lunch and talk over what had happened. A few of the group thought that it was the ideal property, but then everyone turned to me and said it was my decision and that I had the final say. Again, I was being pushed into being a leader, which was a recurring thing in my life. I have never wanted to be the leader or in a prominent position, always quite happy to be part of the crowd or working away in the background, but situations have always pushed me to the front again.

I told them that there was something about the place that made me uneasy, although I couldn't say what. They were surprised, except for the girl who had been with me at the Fogou. We decided to book into a B & B for the night. After our evening meal we were having a drink and chatting when a woman, who was a medium, came over to sit with me. She sat very close to me so that I could hear her above the noise in the bar, and told me urgently that I had to be extremely careful because the energy of the property was ancient and earth-based. It was so strong it had sensed my energy and had called me from Essex. She also told me that 'an entity' would be coming to me that night and that I had to be strong and put up every bit of protection I could. Apparently, this ancient entity wanted not just my energy but my husband's and daughters' too, to work the land there. She also warned me that it only wanted female energy and that there was a history of previous male owners either leaving quickly or coming to harm. She had sensed all this while watching me across the bar.

As you can imagine, I was terrified at what I might have done to my family and grateful that I had listened to my intuition concerning the place. You can also imagine my fear of going up to my room alone, not knowing what might be waiting for me in the dark! Even to this day when I think about that time I am still amazed at how brave I was. I said goodnight to the rest of the group and made my way up to my room, asking the angels to put their protection around me as I opened my door and stepped into the pitch blackness of the room, while trying to find the light switch. To my great relief the light came on and my room was as I had left it, with nothing nasty in sight. I sat on the bed and asked what I should do to protect myself in the best possible way, and an image flashed into my mind of me having a shower. I got the impression this was to wash off any residual energy from the property. Then I had an image of my deck of angel cards and remembered they were in my case - I had brought them with me to give readings to the group, if asked.

So I had a shower, visualising any residual energy washing off me and going down the plug hole. Once I was dry and had my pyjamas on, I lay on top of the bed propped up by the pillows, then spread my angel cards in a circle around me asking for protection during the night. I thought I had better switch off the main light and just have the bedside lamp on, because I wanted to show 'the entity' that I was not afraid of it coming to me (although my poor heart was beating fast). I stayed alert until about two in the morning but then my eyes began to close and I fell asleep.

I woke up with a start at about six-thirty, and as I looked at a patch of carpet near my bed, I saw a pair of feet materialising, followed by a pair of hairy legs that had leather thongs going up them from leather sandals. As I continued to watch, fascinated, the hem of a tartan kilt appeared above the legs. I was watching someone materialise from the feet upwards. At that point I said, "Oh, go away. You're too late now!" and everything disappeared, leaving the musky smell of wet wool behind.

When I went down to breakfast later, the group all looked hesitantly at me to see how I was. The medium had told them what she told me, and some of them were angry at her for letting me face it alone. Everyone was relieved when they saw that I was all right and asked me what had happened. I told them what I'd done and what I'd seen that morning. The girl who had bought the book from Tim gave a gasp and asked me if I had read the book yet. I said I hadn't had time, so she told me that she had read it during the night; in the book Tim mentioned a 'protector' who manifests as a red-headed Scotsman in a woollen kilt. I had sent the good guy away!

Before we left, the medium came over to me to apologise if she had upset me. I told her not to worry as I hadn't been upset, and she smiled. She then whispered to me that the entity had sensed that my energy was as strong as its own, so it had chosen to back off. I was very relieved to hear that, I can tell you. After a weekend of adventure, we all went back home and I just told my husband that we had decided the property wasn't for us.

Reading through the last few chapters myself, I realise that my husband comes across as someone unsympathetic to my beliefs, but I want to put the record straight. Although he wasn't happy with some of the things I did, he always supported me in any way he could. He never stopped me from doing what I needed to do, even if it meant I had to go away for weekends, such as for training. He would take care of the girls and make sure life continued as normal for them. As I have already mentioned, I am not good with computers so he built my website and was always happy to help our friends and my Reiki clients with any computer problems. He also had a great sense of humour. One evening, one of my male Reiki clients was leaving as my husband came into the hallway. After the client had gone he turned to me and said, "I must be a very trusting or a very gullible husband." I asked him why and his response was, "Well, strange men come to the house. You take them upstairs for an hour and then they come back down smiling and giving you money. I assume it is only Reiki you're doing up there?" I laughingly reassured him.

I knew that he was a spiritual person too but he never acknowledged it. We were telepathic, as are many couples who have been together for a long time, and it would drive the girls crazy when we could just look at each other and start laughing. I would have made a quip in my head and he would have heard it! Sometimes we played psychic games. We would all link hands and I would send an image out and see who could pick it up. The family were all good at seeing whatever I sent. Another game we played was with a deck of playing cards. We took it in turns trying to predict whether it would be a red or black card turned over, and then what suit it would be. My husband was brilliant at this.

When I became a volunteer on the Community Committee, his reaction was that if you are going to do any work then you should get paid for it. "Volunteering is a mug's game." But little by little I roped him into helping out at the public events the committee organised. He was in charge of the snow machine that was bought by the committee, and every year it snowed on the nativity scene involving local school children in the shelter of the church gate. As we were the ones storing the machine, we were allowed to use it ourselves on Christmas Eve, so it always snowed in our front garden. We used to hide behind the bedroom curtains while the machine sent snow out into the garden, and watch the expressions on people's faces as they went past!

In the end, my husband became more and more involved with the committee and it was lovely to go to meetings together and have an input. One day we were both attending a workshop on how to take minutes at a meeting. The lady running it suddenly turned to me and said, "Are you the Reiki lady?" My husband found it amusing that Reiki could even come up at a boring minute-taking workshop. Then much to everyone's surprise, including his own, he changed his career entirely from being a photographic printer to a Community Development Officer with a local council. His job involved working with the voluntary sector and local deprived communities, and he absolutely loved it. He was a champion for volunteers and always said they were the backbone of any organisation and should be given every oppor-tunity of free training in return for the work they did.

You can imagine the irony when he was invited to tea at Buckingham Palace with some of his volunteer colleagues. This was the man who had said that volunteering was a mug's game, and there he was having tea with the Queen and Prince Philip...

It was a terrible shock for everyone when he died suddenly, at work in front of his colleagues. We were told later that he'd had a massive heart attack and died instantly – a lovely way to go, but awful for those of us left behind. I'm happy to say that I have received lots of messages from him through medium friends and strangers, and I have talked to him in dreams. He even told me that he had met our first grandchild in the spirit world and was waiting for her to join us here on Earth. My elder daughter gave birth to a beautiful little girl; I am a very proud granny and I know my husband watches over her and loves her too.

A few months ago at a Reiki Share, Maggie told me that 'him-self' (as she liked to call him) had been with us. She said that he had stood in front of her morphing his face to make her laugh while she was channelling Reiki to one of the group. She told him to stop it as she had to concentrate. He then stood with his arm around a lady that Maggie recognised as her recently deceased mother-in-law. My husband told Maggie that the lady was fine and that 'they' now had her. This was very comforting to Maggie.

While she was telling the group this, one of the younger ladies looked shocked and asked his name, so I told her and asked why. She said that she never sees anything when channelling Reiki, but this time a man had suddenly appeared in front of her. She had asked him who he was and he gave his name. She then asked him why was he there and he told her it was to protect us all. Someone else also said that she had felt someone gently blowing in her face. All this activity and I wasn't aware of it!

CHAPTER ELEVEN

Astral Projection

One of the ways to use Reiki is to 'send' it to someone if they can't physically get to you. When I first started to do this, a strange thing sometimes happened.

My friend at the Minor Injury Unit wasn't feeling too well and asked if I could send her some Reiki one evening. At the specified time, I went up to my bedroom, lit a candle and tuned in to the energy. As I focussed on my friend, I started to see in my mind a bedroom. The wallpaper was pale with little pink flowers on it. I saw a white wardrobe and then my friend lying in bed with her eyes closed. This had not happened to me before and I wondered what was going on. The next day I rang my friend to see how she was, and she said she was feeling much better. Out of curiosity, I asked her if she had pale wallpaper with little pink flowers on it in her bedroom. She spluttered and asked me how I knew. I told her and her response was, "Crikey, does that mean I shall have to be decent when you send it?"

Some time later another friend asked if I could send healing to her father-in-law. He had come back from a foreign holiday and was now very ill in hospital. Of course I said I would, and that night I started to send Reiki to this man. I had met him a few times at my friend's house so I could picture him in my head. As I did this, I found myself suddenly sitting next to his bed in the hospital. The lights were dim as it was late at night. I put my hand on top of his, which was resting on the covers, and we started to communicate telepathically. I then watched as a light shone from the bottom of his bed – I thought it was a nurse shining a torch on him to see if he was all right, but when I looked there was nobody there. The light became thin and concentrated, like a laser beam, and scanned him from the feet upwards to above his head, and then back down to his feet again. I then heard in my head that it was time to go. It felt important to notice what pyjamas he was wearing, and then I was back in my bedroom again. I rushed downstairs to tell my husband what had happened and to tell him that this man had been wearing blue and white striped pyjamas. My poor husband didn't know what to make of this!

When my friend came round for coffee the next day I told her that I had seen her father-in-law and had ended up sitting next to his bed on the ward. She laughed but I didn't think she believed me, so I told her about the blue and white striped pyjamas. She frowned and said that he only had two pairs of pyjamas, one olive green and the other a pale blue with dark blue piping (she and her husband had bought them for him to have in hospital as he didn't usually wear anything in bed). I was still sure they were blue and white striped ones that I had seen so we left it at that. The following day she knocked on my door and told me that she had just been up to visit her father-in-law and he was wearing his green pyjamas. She had asked him if he wanted any washing done and he said there was some in his locker. To her amazement, when she opened the locker there were the blue and white striped pyjamas that someone else had brought in for him and which he had worn the night I had sent Reiki. It was fantastic to have confirmation that I had actually seen him.

On another occasion I was asked by my best friend if I could do anything to help her dad. He was in hospital with kidney problems. That night, once again, I was sitting in my bedroom and focussing on him and before I knew it I was standing at the entrance to the hospital. In my head I asked where he was and I was instantly facing the Renal Unit building, so I focussed on an image of him and suddenly I was standing at the foot of his bed. Again it was late at night and only a soft glow of light showed in his room. He was connected to lots of machines and tubes and I could hear the bleeping of the monitor.

As I stood at the end of his bed sending him Reiki, he suddenly 'sent' me an image of a young man with black hair and a leather jacket, standing next to a motorbike. This told me that he wanted his loved ones to remember him as this healthy man and not the sick man he had become. I promised him I would tell them and then suddenly I was back in my room again. The next day I asked my friend if her dad had black hair and a motorbike when he was younger. She went very quiet and asked me how I knew this. I told her what I'd seen and that he wanted to be remembered as he once was and not as he was now. My friend couldn't believe this had happened and was expecting a 'phone call to say her dad had died. A week or so later I was talking to a mutual friend who asked me if I had heard the news about our friend's dad. I was dreading to hear that he had passed away, but in fact he had been discharged from hospital because he had made a remarkable recovery. I was so relieved. Sadly, he passed away two years later but I'm sure he had sorted out all his unfinished business with his loved ones by then.

My mum is one of six children but she and her big sister are the only ones alive. When her youngest brother died, my aunt asked me if I would come to the funeral as she felt she might need some Reiki to help her through the day. I went with my parents and after the service we all went back to my cousin's house for food. My aunt found me an hour later and said it was all right to use my cousin's bedroom to give her some Reiki, so up we went. She sat on the dressing table stool and closed her eyes, while I stood behind her and connected to the energy. After about ten minutes I opened my eyes to see how she was. To my surprise, just in front of us, a pair of 'winkle picker' boots materialised on the floor. My aunt still had her eyes closed, which meant she had drifted off to somewhere nice, so I continued to watch the floor. Once the boots had become clear, a pair of light coloured jeans appeared and then my uncle became totally visible, not looking the age he was when he died but more like in his thirties. He had both his thumbs tucked into his belt and he was smiling at me.

In my head, I asked him if there was a message for my aunt and he replied, "Tell her you saw me looking like this and that I want her to remember me like this and not how I was in the end," and then he disappeared. By then the Reiki had stopped flowing and my aunt started to come back from wherever she was. She opened her eyes and smiled and said how much better she was now feeling. I told her what I had seen and as I described what my uncle was wearing she gasped, telling me that there was a photograph at her home in which he is wearing exactly the same clothes, taken when he was in his thirties. She felt so much better after hearing his message and I was amazed that once again I had got confirmation of what I had seen.

Not long after I had my Reiki training, I noticed that the National Federation of Spiritual Healers was holding its annual conference somewhere in the north. It was the last day to apply for tickets to attend and I was sure I'd left it too late to get a place. Although I wasn't a Spiritualist healer myself, I was interested in finding out what the difference was in our methods. A few days later, much to my surprise, my ticket arrived through the post and then I was on a coach heading north, gazing out of the window at the green rolling hills passing by. The more north the coach travelled, the more the big white fluffy clouds in the blue sky seemed to get closer to the ground. I thought this was strange but continued to gaze out at the scenery. Suddenly a 'door' appeared in the cloud closest to the coach and a rainbow 'river' began to pour out and flow down like a waterfall. As I continued watching, fascinated, the river of colour then flowed along parallel to the coach. I couldn't believe my eyes and wanted to ask the lady sitting in the seat behind me if she could see this too, but I didn't want to be seen as the mad woman on the coach! The rainbow river continued to flow down the side of the cloud for another few miles and then began to fade until it was gone. I took this as a good omen for the weekend conference.

Although I wasn't a Spiritualist, I was made to feel welcome by the organisers. One of the workshops was on Aura Soma, which is about colour, oils and essences. Beautiful crystal bottles have different colours – sometimes two in the same bottle – and they are prevented from mixing by a slight film of clear oil. A trained Aura Soma practitioner can give a reading by looking at the colours in the bottles that you have chosen.

One of the ladies who attended the workshop was partially sighted so I helped her to a seat next to mine. I admit to wondering how she would benefit as she wouldn't be able to see very much. The lady running the workshop had put all her bottles on the windowsill of the room and the sun made them sparkle – it was a beautiful sight. She explained that people were drawn to the colours that were lacking in their aura; they would not be aware that this was the reason they chose a particular bottle, but would be drawn intuitively to what they needed. She then told us of a few cases where the colour in the bottle had been taken out just by somebody holding the bottle, someone who desperately needed the colour. I doubted this – how could the colour become clear while still in the bottle?

She asked us to go over to the windowsill and choose the bottle we were most drawn to, hold it in our hands and take it back to our seat. I helped the partially sighted lady over to the bottles and she just put her hand out and felt them until she found one that she liked. It was a deep sky blue. She clutched it in her hand while we made our way back to our seats where, to my astonishment, as she put the bottle down on the table I saw that it had gone clear. There was no sign of the colour that had been in there. It was as if the spirit world was saying to me (yet again), "You WILL believe this." The lady who had chosen it was feeling so much better that she didn't want to hand it back, so she ended up buying the bottle.

The bottle I had chosen meant that I was 'a messenger, feet on the earth and head in Heaven, a gatherer and giver of information'. We were then asked to put the bottles back and choose one more, and when back in our seats we were to hold the bottle in our palms and see what we could pick up. After helping the lady with me to find hers, I chose mine and sat back down, holding it in my hands as directed. The strangest sensations started in my hands and I felt the bottle get colder and colder until it was too painful for me to hold anymore. While this was going on I was trying to get images from the bottle but nothing came, just complete pitch blackness.

The lady running the workshop then went around each of us asking what we had seen and felt while holding our bottle. I was beginning to worry as my experience had been totally different to others' and I was convinced I had done something wrong. When she got to me, she crouched down next to me and asked what I had experienced. I shook my head and apologised that I had not done it properly because I had only seen pitch blackness and the bottle had got so cold that I'd had to put it down. She rocked back on her heels and looked at me in a strange way, then said that I had, in fact, been in the presence of God. The blackness was the vastness of the universe; she also explained that when the spirit is close the temperature drops, and that was why the bottle had got painfully cold – I was in the presence of God! She seemed quite shocked, but no more than I was.

While at this conference I made friends with another lady and on the last afternoon we bought raffle tickets for a draw that was being held, the prizes having been donated by members. The draw was held in the big lecture room with tiered seats. As my friend and I walked past the table with the prizes on it, I noticed a book that I had wanted to read. My friend was about to walk up to the top tier of seats but I called her back to sit in the third row instead. She asked why, and I said that I didn't want to have to walk too far when I went up to collect the book! The third ticket drawn was mine, and the look of surprise on my friend's face made me laugh as I walked the short distance to collect my prize.

CHAPTER TWELVE

The Extraordinary (Part 2)

I am so grateful for all the weird and wonderful stuff that has happened in my life. It certainly hasn't been dull.

A few years ago I joined a society that included psychiatrists and psychotherapists, as well as healers of all types. This organisation understood about souls being trapped on the Earth plane and about 'attachments', where a soul might attach itself to something familiar such as a person or even a piece of furniture. The psychiatric world was slowly beginning to understand some of these reasons for mental problems.

I attended a conference one year held at Regent's Park in London and Pat came as my guest. There were many well-known speakers in their fields and towards the end of the afternoon they held a Question-and-Answer session with the delegates. They were interested in people's experiences of soul attachment. I raised my hand three times to share my experience about a client's dead husband, but each time the microphone went past me. After the third time I just shrugged and said to Pat that I obviously wasn't meant to share it. There was a short break before the closing of the conference, so Pat and I wandered off to take a look at some of the stalls set up in another room. I was drawn to a book stall and while there started chatting with the lady who ran it. I laughingly told her about not being picked to share my experience but she was very interested; apparently a journalist friend of hers had asked her to look out for any interesting stories while at the conference. She asked if she might take my 'phone number and name so that she could pass it on to her friend. I gave them to her and then it was time to go back for the closing ceremony.

Afterwards a group of us decided to go to the cafe in Regent's Park before heading home. While pouring out the tea for the people on my table, I chatted about the day and the things we had learned, and I asked the man opposite if he was a psychiatrist. He answered, "No, I am a biophysicist and I'm lecturing around the world as of tomorrow." He was fascinating to listen to, but he had to leave early as he still had to do his packing.

On the way home I had a call from the journalist, who was freelance but wanted to write about me for the Daily Mirror. When I got home I asked the girls and my husband what they had been up to that day. Once they had told me, I said, "Well, I'm going to be interviewed for the Daily Mirror newspaper and I had tea with a biophysicist in Regent's Park!" A photographer came down from London to take my picture for the article and it came out a few weeks later - my dad was so proud, as he is an avid reader of the Daily Mirror.

A while ago, at a healing festival, two psychics told me that I should work in the media but I was horrified and said, "No thank you." However, once I was home I had to kick myself – I already am involved with the media. I write articles for the magazine of my Reiki Guild, and I have co-authored a book with Maggie (on the menopause); I have also been in newspapers and magazines and on the local radio, so all I need now is my own TV show and that will be all areas of the media covered!

The Extraordinary (Part 2)

Before I moved to Somerset, I wrote an article about energising water by the Dr Emoto method and sent it to my Reiki Guild. A few weeks later I had a 'phone call one evening from what sounded like an elderly gentleman. He said he was very interested in the article I had published in the Dowsers' Society magazine. I was puzzled because I had never heard of this, and the gentleman was also surprised that I was a woman because he'd assumed Chris Guyon was a man. So you can imagine the confusion that reigned at the beginning of our conversation. He went on to tell me his name, that he was eighty-three years old and that he had worked with the spirit world for many years. He knew that this was his last incarnation and that he would be going 'home' when he passed. He told me a lot about dowsing and why he had been interested in my article.

Then he said he could sense that my energy was quite low: my level was 'only at a four when it should have been eight'. He said he would bring my energy up to seven and told me to sit still while he sent the energy. To be honest, I didn't feel any different but then he said, "You're sitting in your kitchen at a wooden table aren't you?" I confirmed this was true. He said he was sending the energy into the wooden table, to anchor it in my home; at that moment my poor cat Gabriel leapt up in fright from where he'd been lying on the table and jumped to the floor. So I couldn't doubt that something had happened that time.

When I later moved to my present home, I joined a psychic development circle and after a few years happened to mention there the 'phone call from the elderly gentleman. The lady who ran the circle looked amazed and so did a few of the regular members. They told me that I had described exactly one of the circle's members who had died a few years ago. How amazing is that? He contacted me years before I even thought about moving house and he was a member of the same circle I was eventually to join.

Another interesting person I met after I'd moved is Carol Pearce, who runs her own healing practice called The Changist. She attends circle too but is now a student of Dr Harry Oldfield;

he has invented many things over his career but the latest is NEV software[5] that shows human energy in real time. Carol is working with him in using this technology to show the body's meridian lines (as seen by ancient mystics) and the human energy field. Carol also uses NEV to help the clients she sees in her practice. Dr Oldfield's dream is that every doctor's surgery will have a NEV machine as a diagnostic tool in the near future. One of the other interesting things it can show, apparently, is spirit energy and images of the past imprinted on the present. Fascinating! I have had the privilege of being a guinea pig in some of the experiments with NEV and Carol has also given talks at my home for those who wanted to know more about what she was doing.

I have always loved crystals and started to collect them many years before I started my spiritual path. One night I was having a lovely dream when I was suddenly taken out of it and found myself in a long corridor with a shelf running along the wall at shoulder height on the left. Just as I was wondering what was going on, I saw two young men walking towards me. One was carrying something that looked about the size of a football but was covered by a gold cloth. As they reached me they said, "Remember, the first got broken." I wasn't what they were referring to but then the gold cloth was lifted and I saw that it was a huge crystal. Again I was told, "Remember, the first was broken, take care." Then they said what sounded like, "Step du moliere – write it down, you will forget. Step du moliere." They then passed the crystal to me and as they did so I woke up. I quickly found my pen and pad by the bed and wrote down what they had said.

The next morning I had a call from the medium whose circle I sat in. I told her what I had seen and she said that she was sitting in front of her computer so would look online for "Step du moliere". She asked me how was it spelled but I said I didn't know – I had written it phonetically to remind me in the morning. I also told her

---

[5]   New Energy Vision. There are details for contacting Carol Pearce and Dr Oldfield at the end of this book.

that it wouldn't be rocket science, otherwise they wouldn't have entrusted this crystal to me! She then said, "Chris, it is science. Moliere was the scientist who discovered the energy of crystals - it's just come up on my screen." I didn't know who was more shocked with this information. So apparently I have the energy of this crystal in my system, to be used at some time in the future. I must also remember that "The first was broken." It feels like a very big responsibility, but I shall carry it until the time comes for it to be used.

I love the look and feel of crystals and have had some fascinating results when using them in a healing capacity. My husband had to go through a long drawn-out court case (nothing that he had done wrong) and had to travel to London every time. He was very stressed out with the case and with the travelling so one day I suggested that he took one of my rose quartz crystals with him. He looked at me as if I was mad but I suggested he just put it in his jacket pocket, and every time he felt overwhelmed he was to hold it. He took the crystal with a rise of his eyebrows, but when he came home later that day he confessed that he had felt it very comforting to hold it while in court.

I remember getting a book on crystals and their healing properties out of the local library and decided to try some of the things suggested in it. My elder daughter was happy to be my guinea pig so she sat in the chair while I gave her different crystals to hold. I stood behind her with the book to see what I had to do, and what surprised us both was that my daughter was describing exactly what the book said she should feel. I also love the crystal wands that are for sale at Mind Body and Spirit exhibitions but have never been able to afford one.

I have already mentioned Dr Emoto's work with water and after seeing his talk I felt full of inspiration that this was something the Reiki Share group could get involved with. At the next Share night I told the group about the talk and I described how to energise the jug of water we had.

Then, a few months later, the terrible conditions of the refugee camps in Darfur were on the news. I had been sending Reiki to their situation but had a nagging feeling that something more could be done. On the day of Reiki Share I had been watching the news and saw that cholera had broken out at the camps and people were dying for the lack of fresh water. I then heard my guides tell me to 'send' healing water to the camps. All they would show me was a tray with tumblers on and a pitcher of water. That evening I told the group what I had been shown to do but said I still had no idea how to do it. The group trusted me and were happy to go along with whatever I was shown. So a tray was brought in with tumblers and a large glass pitcher of water, and placed on the coffee table in the middle of the room. I then asked my guides to show me what to do. It was like looking at a video playing just in front of my eyes. I was shown that we were to energise the water by placing our hands on the glass pitcher and saying three times:

> *Water we love you.*
> *Water we honour you.*
> *Water we respect you.*

As we did this, the temperature of the water started to drop and in the end it was too cold for us to keep our hands on it. I was then shown the pitcher pouring water into the tumblers, so that's what we did. Once we all had a full tumbler I was then shown us drinking it with the intention of having pure water in the camps. It was explained to me that everything is made of molecules, and as we drank the energised water it would come out through the molecules of the body and 'surf' all the molecules of the air until it reached the stagnant and filthy ponds and streams at Darfur. As the molecules touched this water it would start to run clear and clean. I 'saw' a group of refugees standing around a stagnant pond in despair, and then watched as the water turned crystal clear and blue. The people were literally jumping for joy as the water became drinkable.

When we had all finished drinking the water we looked at each other in amazement. We took it in turns to share what we had witnessed and we had all seen the filthy water turn clean and pure. I wrote to the Red Cross who were running the camp and told them what we had done as a Reiki group, saying that I knew it was probably hard for their fieldworkers to believe but asking if they would let us know if the water situation changed. Sadly I never received a reply, but from that day on there were no more news reports about the cholera situation in Darfur.

CHAPTER THIRTEEN

And Finally *(for now)*

One day, when I was working at my first job at the dental surgery, I popped out at lunchtime to do a quick spot of shopping. Luckily, where I worked was close to a large shopping centre. Even though I rushed round I was worried about getting back late for work. To get to the surgery, I had to cross a major roundabout where buses passed frequently. In my panic to get back to work, I judged that the distance between me and the next bus coming along was just enough for me to run across, but as I started to dash across the busy road my foot was caught and I tripped. As I went sprawling into the road I looked up to see the shocked face of the bus driver, because he and I knew that he was about to run me over. At that precise moment, I felt as if someone was picking me up and I was thrown across to the other side of the road just as the bus reached me. I scrambled to my feet wanting to thank the person who had saved me but no-one was there. I knew that I was very lucky to be alive and I thanked my angel for saving me. Since then I never take risks when crossing a busy road…

Years later I was living in a different area and working at a different dental surgery. I could walk to work which was great as my husband and I were trying to save up for a deposit on a house. Once again I had to cross a very busy road to get to work but I always made sure I was safe before crossing. One day I waited for a car transporter to go past before crossing. When I was halfway across, one of the cars on the top tier of the transporter broke free and slid off, fell onto the road and then bounced towards me… It was so surreal, everything in slow motion, and I stood transfixed by the sight of this car bouncing towards me when once again I was given a massive shove which propelled me to the other side of the road, just as the car came to a skidding halt at the spot where I'd been standing.

You would think that I'd be wary of car transporters after that, but I assumed it was just 'one of those things' that happen once in a lifetime. Yet a few years later I was driving to see my parents and at a roundabout there was a car transporter in front of me, just pulling onto the roundabout. As I began to move forward, I heard a loud snapping noise and to my horror one of the cars came loose and fell back into the road, almost causing a serious accident. Thankfully I had kept my distance, already paying attention to my intuition that something wasn't right.

I am lucky still to be friends with girls whom I met at senior school. We would meet up for an evening meal every three months or so to catch up. Some years ago I was on my way to meet them at a country pub, looking forward to the evening. It had started to drizzle, not enough to use the windscreen wipers but enough to distort my vision slightly if cars came towards me with their headlights on full beam, as the light refracted across the windscreen. It was dark and I was driving along a country road, getting a bit nervous about my road position and not sure if I had drifted too close to the centre. A car came towards me with its full beam on and the light just flashed across my windscreen. I turned the steering wheel sharply to the left but unfortunately I had over-compensated, and at sixty miles an hour I crashed into concrete slabs that had been put down only that day at the edge of the road.

Just before I hit the concrete slabs I checked my rear view mirror and saw another car further behind me. The steering wheel was wrenched out of my hands and the car started to spin round and round. I braced myself for the impact of the car behind as it had nowhere to go other than into me. I felt calm and realised that I would not be going home that night, and I thought of my husband and the girls. But the impact never came and the car slowly stopped spinning until it came to rest, facing the right way. Shakily I looked in my mirror to see what had happened to the car behind me, but there was nothing there. To my surprise, the car engine was still running and I carefully put it into gear and set off on the rest of the journey to meet up with my friends.

When I arrived they were very concerned because I was so pale - they thought I'd seen a ghost. I told them what had happened and they were even more worried and offered to buy me a brandy, which I had to decline. At the end of the evening they all waited to make sure the car would start again, and when it did they hugged me goodbye and told me to take it slowly on the way home. I told my husband what had happened and he was only concerned that I was all right and not hurt in any way. I assured him I was fine and we went to bed. The next day he inspected the car and called me to have a look. The front wheel shaft was bent, and he asked me how I'd been able to drive the car when it was so damaged. Even the mechanic who looked at it couldn't believe that I'd managed to drive home. I knew it was my angels looking after me, keeping me safe from my own stupidity in going too fast on a wet night.

When I still lived in Essex I attended an angel conference and went along with one of my friends from the Reiki Share group. There were about two hundred delegates and well-known speakers. The first half of the day was really interesting and my friend and I were having a great time. When it came to the lunch break, I was approached by one of the organisers of the event who asked if I would be prepared to give a talk in the afternoon. I was shocked and asked him why was he asking me as I was only a delegate, but he told me that lots of people were saying they wanted to hear me talk. I still couldn't understand why, but out of my mouth came a 'yes'.

My friend looked at me in amazement and said, "Crikey, rather you than me, girl. I'll send you lots of Reiki while you're up there." He was just as shocked as I was. Of course, I couldn't enjoy my lunch as my stomach was churning at the thought of it. After we were all back in the conference hall, the organiser came over and told me that I would be the first speaker of the afternoon and then he informed the rest of the delegates of a slight change in the running order. Then he introduced me and I made my way to the stage, knees trembling and pleading with my angels not to desert me in my hour of need. It was terrifying looking out at a sea of people, all looking back at me, without a clue about what I was to say. I looked towards my friend and saw that he had his eyes closed and was sending me Reiki to keep me calm. I opened my mouth and the words just spilled out. Part of me was thinking, "Where's this coming from? I know it's not me." While I spoke I could hear people sobbing and the healers in the room went to look after them.

Eventually I could feel my talk naturally coming to an end; I didn't realise at the time that I'd been talking for about twenty minutes. I finished by saying, "And that's what I feel." The hall was so quiet you could hear a pin drop and then it erupted into a standing ovation. I made my way back to my seat in a daze and saw my friend grinning from ear to ear. He gave me a hug as I sat down and told me how proud he was of me. When we got to the afternoon break, I had so many people come up and tell me that what I'd said had touched them. Sadly, I had no idea what I'd said but was grateful that it had meant something to them. Others came and told me that they never normally saw energies but had seen angels around me. One lady said she had seen a figure all in gold with what looked like an Egyptian hairstyle, standing behind me with its hand on my shoulder the whole time I was talking. I was so grateful for their feedback, because then it made sense to me who was doing the talking...

Angels still play a big part in my life now, for which I am extremely grateful, so I shall end this book with a recent angel event. A little while ago I had been to the shops by car and was setting off home again. The car park is in a one-way system and there were some roadworks going on there too. Not wanting to get caught up in the traffic jam they were causing, I decided to drive out of town intending to double back by a different route. After a while I was relieved to see a left turn back towards town, but it was a narrow single track road with steep banks and the hedges were so high that I couldn't see over them. I approached a bend and slowed down but then to my horror saw two cars approaching, with no passing place on either side. I steered towards the hedge on my side to let them pass, but as I did so I heard a loud bang and then a slow hissing noise... Then I suddenly realised that I didn't have my mobile 'phone with me because I'd thought I was just popping to the shops.

The first car went past and for a split second I made eye contact with the driver of the second car. He slowed down and indicated for me to move forward as there was a wider space around the next bend, then he reversed to park off the road in front of me. He got out of his car and walked back up the road, returning with my hub cap and asking if I wanted him to put it back on. Although I was a woman on my own, I didn't feel threatened by his presence and got out of the car to see what had made the noise.

Well, not only did I have a flat tyre but there was a big dent in the wheel itself. We walked back to where it had happened and saw that in the bank underneath the hedge there was a big boulder - when I had steered towards the hedge my wheel had hit this.

This total stranger then just rolled up his sleeves, took off the damaged wheel and put my spare one on so that I could get home safely. I was so grateful that someone in this day and age still knew how to change a wheel, but he just laughed and said he had plenty of practice with his son's car! Once the wheel was on he gave me directions for how to get back to town the safe way and then he drove off.

As I sat in my car I thought how lucky I had been. Without my 'phone I wouldn't have been able to call for assistance and I didn't even know exactly where I was to tell anyone where to find me. I knew that the angels had intervened and impressed on that lovely man that I was in trouble. Maybe he was an Earth angel, sent to make sure I was safe? Whatever the reason, I know my angels were taking care of me as they always have done and always will.

If you haven't connected with your own angels yet, then let my story be the trigger for you to do so. You never know when you might need them!

Contacts

Carol Pearce	*www.thechangist.co.uk*
Dr Masaru Emoto	*http://masaru-emoto.net/english/news.html*
Dr Harry Oldfield	*www.electrocrystal.com*
Oldfield Systems	*www.newenergyvision.co.uk*

Lightning Source UK Ltd.
Milton Keynes UK
UKOW05f1924060614

233024UK00006B/114/P